WITH A SNARL HE RUSHED FORWARD TO TOPPLE THE
LADDER ON WHICH NANCY SWAYED.

The Sign of the Twisted Candles.   *Page 204*

TO NANCY'S HORROR HE HURLED HIS BURDEN FULL
AT MR. HILL.

The Sign of the Twisted Candles.

Page 137

AS SEMITT JAMMED ON HIS BRAKES, HIS SPEEDING CAR
CRASHED INTO A BARB-WIRE FENCE.

The Sign of the Twisted Candles.   *Page 74*

"I GUESS WE'LL HAVE TO RUN FOR IT!" SAID NANCY.

The Sign of the Twisted Candles. *Frontispiece (Page 4)*

NANCY DREW MYSTERY STORIES

THE SIGN OF THE TWISTED CANDLES

BY

CAROLYN KEENE

AUTHOR OF THE SECRET OF THE OLD CLOCK,
THE MYSTERY AT LILAC INN,
THE CLUE IN THE DIARY,
NANCY'S MYSTERIOUS LETTER, ETC.

ILLUSTRATED BY
RUSSELL H. TANDY

WITH AN INTRODUCTION BY
CAROLYN G. HART

FACSIMILE EDITION

BEDFORD, MASSACHUSETTS
APPLEWOOD BOOKS

139941

For further information about these editions, please write:
Applewood Books, Box 365, Bedford, MA 01730.

LIBRARY OF CONGRESS CATALOGING-IN-PUBLICATION DATA
Keene, Carolyn.
    The sign of the twisted candles / by Carolyn Keene;
illustrated by Russell H. Tandy; with an introduction by
Carolyn G. Hart. —Facsimile ed.
        p.   cm.   — (Nancy Drew mystery stories)
    Summary: While solving the mystery of an old man's
disappearing fortune, Nancy ends a family feud and reveals
the identity of an orphan of unknown parentage.
    ISBN 1-55709-163-3
    [1. Mystery and detective stories.]   I. Tandy, Russell
H., ill.   II. Title.   III. Series: Keene, Carolyn. Nancy Drew
mystery stories.
PZ7.K23Sih   1996   J
[Fic]—dc20   96-28382
                            KEE   CIP
                                                        AC

10 9 8 7 6

PUBLISHER'S NOTE

Much has changed in America since the Nancy Drew series first began in 1930. The modern reader may be delighted with the warmth and exactness of the language, the wholesome innocence of the characters, their engagement with the natural world, or the nonstop action without the use of violence; but just as well, the modern reader may be extremely uncomfortable with the racial and social stereotyping, the roles women play in these books, or the use of phrases or situations which may conjure up some response in the modern reader that was not felt by the reader of the times.

For good or bad, we Americans have changed quite a bit since these books were first issued. Many readers will remember these editions with great affection and will be delighted with their return; others will wonder why we just don't let them disappear. These books are part of our heritage. They are a window on our real past. For that reason, except for the addition of this note and the introduction by Carolyn G. Hart, we are presenting *The Sign of the Twisted Candles* unedited and unchanged from its first edition.

Applewood Books

PROMISES KEPT

By
CAROLYN G. HART

AUTHOR OF
DEAD MAN'S ISLAND;
MINT JULEP MURDER;
"DEATH ON DEMAND" MYSTERIES;
& OTHERS

GROWING UP, I knew I could count on these truths:

August meant sunshine, the rasp of cicadas, lemonade in huge, ice-filled glasses.

The start of school meant new clothes, the smell of chalk, reunions with friends.

Newspapers smelled like ink, and big black headlines indicated important events.

And always, *always*, a Nancy Drew mystery invited me to adventure, excitement, and sheer delight.

If I could ever experience again the sense of anticipation I felt when I bought that familiar yellow book, I would be thrilled beyond measure. But the wonder and glory of Nancy Drew's adventures are meant especially for the young. I won't ever thrill to any mystery the way I did to *The Secret of the Old Clock* or *The Clue in the Diary*, but it was an enormous pleasure to read again *The Sign of the Twisted Candles* and to remember the joy I felt so long ago.

The Sign of the Twisted Candles is, of course, vintage Nancy Drew. It includes all the elements that have delighted generations of readers:

Nancy Drew, an independent, capable, and thoughtful heroine.

Her father, Carson Drew, who respects his daughter and encourages her independence.

Hannah Gruen, the housekeeper for the Drews and a comforting support for the motherless Nancy.

Cousins Bess Marvin and George Fayne, Nancy's best friends in River Heights. Bess is quite fond of extra snacks and George is always ready for adventure and both Bess and George follow Nancy's lead.

In common with all the Nancy Drew mysteries, *The Sign of the Twisted Candles* has moments of great danger for Nancy and plenty of opportunities for her to exercise leadership. *The Sign of the Twisted Candles* offers a damsel in distress, interesting facts about the making of candles, and a consideration of where loyalties should lie. Bess and George have family ties to a faction of a warring family and, for a time, they turn their backs on Nancy.

The Sign of the Twisted Candles serves, as do all good mysteries, as a parable. Readers have the chance to assess what may result in their own lives if bitterness and greed are indulged.

There is so much to be gained from this book and from all the Nancy Drew mysteries. One wonderful result may be a lifelong commitment to reading mysteries.

It certainly happened to me. I grew up reading Nancy Drew and the Hardy Boys and Beverly Gray. As a young writer, I read in a magazine for writers about a contest offer for a mystery for girls eight to twelve. I thought, Gee, I loved Nancy Drew. I believe I'll try to write that book. I did. *The Secret of the Cellars* won the contest and was published in 1964. That was my first published book. I wrote several more mysteries for younger readers. My first adult mystery—*Flee from the Past*—was published in 1976. My most recent novel, *Mint Julep Murder*, is my 25th mystery novel to be published.

So I've been involved with mysteries all my life, first as a reader, then as a writer. And that lifelong fascination with mysteries began when I read my first Nancy Drew.

But why mysteries? What is it about the mystery that I admire and that readers, young and old, find absorbing? What makes mysteries the favorite reading of thoughtful readers?

I would point again to the Nancy Drew mysteries.

Why did I love those books? What did I find in those books?

I found independence, a battle for justice, and a puzzle. And I found a world where goodness triumphs. As we all know to our sorrow, this is not true in the real world. In the real world, we are stricken by the evil of the Holocaust, sickened by massacres in Bosnia, appalled by a mind that crafts bombs to mail to innocent recipients.

But in the mystery, justice prevails. The mystery, in addition to a puzzle and a quest, is a reaffirmation of our faith in goodness. The mystery is a celebration of justice. And that's why I cheer every time I see a young reader with a Nancy Drew mystery. That reader is going to grow up to be a good citizen, a caring citizen.

There are two sharply different kinds of mysteries, the crime novel and the traditional mystery. The crime novel features heroes such as Sam Spade or V.I. Warshawski, and the traditional mystery features the amateur sleuth such as Miss Marple or my own Henrie O.

The crime novel is the story of an honorable woman—or man—who tries to remain uncorrupted in a corrupt world. The crime novel is always the story of the detective's struggle to bring about justice. Today's private eye is the white knight who will never betray her code of honor.

Just like Nancy Drew.

The other great kind of mystery is the traditional mystery. The traditional mystery is at the heart of our lives. It focuses on relationships, what happens when we treat people cruelly, what the future may hold if we are selfish, vain, or arrogant. Or, in the case of *The Sign of the Twisted Candles*, how greed can destroy character.

Agatha Christie once compared the mystery to the medieval morality play. It is a brilliant analogy. In the medieval morality play, the tradesfair audiences saw a graphic presentation of what happens to lives dominated by lust, gluttony, sloth, and all the deadly sins. This is precisely what readers of Nancy Drew mysteries are offered.

The traditional mystery provides readers with parables. In *The Sign of the Twisted Candles*, readers must confront the question of how greed affects lives, greed and an unwillingness to forgive.

In the crime novel, the detective explores how society has been warped and strained by those who flout laws and conventions. Nancy Drew, too, often faces down drug traffickers or chicanery in public office.

In the traditional mystery, the detective searches out the reasons for murder by exploring the relationships between the victim and those around the victim. The detective is trying to find out what caused the turmoil in these lives. What fractured the relationships among these people? Just as Nancy Drew explores the reasons behind the puzzles she encounters.

When readers observe the lives around them, they can see the torment of fractured relationships. Usually these emotional dramas do not end in murder. In fact, they do not end. The violent emotions created by fractured relationships can corrode the lives of every person involved and the bitterness can affect many generations. It is made abundantly clear in *The Sign of the Twisted Candles* just how far-reaching the effects of anger can be.

The traditional mystery focuses on the destructive secrets hidden beneath what so often seems to be a placid surface. In *The Sign of the Twisted Candles*, Nancy Drew isn't content to accept the ordinary surface of life at the Inn. Instead, she delves beneath the surface to discover fraud, cruelty, and greed.

So it is no accident that Nancy Drew captures the hearts and minds of her readers. We would all like to be like Nancy, brave, honorable, righting wrongs.

But her readers also learn much about life in the pages of the Nancy Drew mysteries. They recognize the characters in the books, beset by selfishness, greed, anger, and despair. Oh yes, that's just like the girl in my Spanish class. Or yes, that's just like Aunt Alice. Or the woman across the street. Or me.

Readers are deeply concerned about the expressions of dissension and violence far short of murder that occur in their own lives. Readers know what it is like to be angry with those around them. They know the jealous mother, the miserly uncle, the selfish sister, the impossible teacher. These are the realities of life with which they must cope.

So this is one reason why the Nancy Drew mysteries are so popular. They celebrate the good in our lives—commitment, honesty, caring—and they vanquish the bad—fear, cruelty, and selfishness.

There will always be anger and quarrels. But we can better understand how these emotions destroy lives when we read mysteries.

Mysteries mirror the realities of our lives, personal and social. But the greatest gift we take from the mystery is a continuing reassurance that goodness matters.

In life, evil often triumphs, as we know only too well. But we still want the world to be good, we want the world to be fair, we want the world to be just.

There is a magic place where goodness always triumphs, where justice is served, where wrongs are righted.

Read the Nancy Drew mysteries. Nancy Drew will never disappoint you. I promise.

NANCY DREW MYSTERY STORIES

THE SIGN OF THE TWISTED CANDLES

BY

CAROLYN KEENE

Author of THE SECRET OF THE OLD CLOCK,
THE MYSTERY AT LILAC INN,
THE CLUE IN THE DIARY,
NANCY'S MYSTERIOUS LETTER, ETC.

ILLUSTRATED BY

RUSSELL H. TANDY

NEW YORK

GROSSET & DUNLAP

PUBLISHERS

Made in the United States of America

NANCY DREW
MYSTERY STORIES
By CAROLYN KEENE
12mo. Cloth. Illustrated.

GROSSET & DUNLAP, PUBLISHERS, NEW YORK

The Sign of the Twisted Candles

CONTENTS

iv Contents

THE SIGN OF THE TWISTED CANDLES

CHAPTER I

TRAPPED BY THE TEMPEST

"OH, NANCY! I'm afraid to go any farther, and I'm afraid not to. Won't you speed the car up?"

Nancy Drew smiled grimly to herself, despite the awe-inspiring situation with which she had to battle.

"Which shall it be, Bess? Shall we stop or shall we try to go faster?" Nancy asked the girl beside her in the sporty little roadster.

Bess's answer was drowned out by a peal of thunder which followed a blinding flash of lightning. Nancy cast an apprehensive glance at the sky, where black and lead-colored clouds writhed and twisted, although not a sign of a breeze fluttered the tree leaves along the country road up which the automobile was running.

"Look how yellow the sky is getting in the southwest," exclaimed the third occupant of the car, George Fayne, who, despite the name, was an attractive girl of about the same age as Nancy and Bess Marvin, her cousin.

The three chums had gone for a ride this sultry August afternoon to seek relief from the heat. Some thirty miles from their home town of River Heights, while traversing an unfamiliar cross-road, they had noticed the suddenly darkened sky.

"I guess we are in for it," Nancy cried, as the trees and shrubs bent before a blast of hot wind. A peculiar yellowish tinge spread over the sky, tinting the landscape with a ghostly pallor. Then, without further warning, as if a gigantic bucket had been inverted overhead, the rain poured down in torrents. In a second the road was obscured, and a few minutes later it became a stream in which the wheels, sending sheets of water fender-high, skidded sickeningly.

Nancy had slackened the pace of her car to a crawl.

The thunder was almost continuous now, making conversation impossible. Bess cowered between her companions, her eyes screwed tightly shut, her fingers to her ears. George, too, was pale and tense when the lightning's glare revealed her face.

"Can't we stop under a tree?" she shouted.

"Worst place in the world to pick in a thunderstorm," Nancy cried.

As if in confirmation of her opinion, a bolt of lightning found its mark in a great, arching elm a few rods ahead. In the almost blinding glare the girls saw the huge trunk ripped by a splintering furrow from top to bottom, while twigs and branches went hurtling before the wind.

"My, but that was close," Nancy exclaimed, blinking her blue eyes. "Too close for comfort. Say, George, isn't that a light ahead?"

George peered through the murk.

"It's a house, I'm sure," she cried. "Stop a minute. Here's a signboard. It says: 'Luncheons and dinners served at The Sign of the Twisted Candles fifty feet ahead.'"

"Good. We'll find shelter until the storm blows over," Nancy called out, turning into a driveway which came into view.

As she shifted into second gear the motor sputtered warningly. The car lurched, and a sheet of muddy water deluged the windshield as the front wheels sank more than hub-deep into the rain-gouged gutter of the dirt road. With a last cough the engine stopped.

"Oh, pshaw!" Nancy exclaimed in vexation. "I guess the distributor got wet. We're stuck."

Bess opened her eyes warily and took her fingers from her ears.

"Why did you stop here?" she demanded.

"I didn't stop; I was stopped," Nancy an-

swered ruefully. "I guess we'll have to run
for it. The car is blocking the driveway, but
probably no one will be using this road for a
while."

Gathering their skirts tightly about them,
the girls stepped out onto the running-board
and jumped over the swirling, foam-flecked
current that raced down the side of the road.
Bending their heads before the storm, the trio
dashed for the tea room, revealed now as a
rambling building of the Civil War period, its
central structure a flat-roofed, three-story
tower flanked by long story-and-a-half wings.
There was a dim glow of light from the ground
floor windows, and in the arched window at the
top of the tower a sturdy candle-light gleamed
welcomingly.

Laughing, gasping and almost breathless,
Nancy and her chums scampered up the broad
front steps of the place and onto the wide
porch. An array of tables and chairs had evidently been hastily pushed against the walls.

"I'm sure I look a fright," Bess panted.

"None of us looks especially like a page from
a fashion magazine," Nancy laughed, running
her slim fingers through her wavy, blond hair.
"Who would expect us to, when we've just
barely escaped from drowning?"

Nancy led the way to the door and opened
it without ceremony. The three girls found
themselves in a long hall, lighted by curiously

twisted candles in sconces on the walls. To the left and to the right arched doorways opened into high-ceilinged rooms where tables, each with a candle fluttering in the draft, were set in rows. Half a dozen couples looked up curiously as the girls entered, and then resumed their contemplation of food or storm.

From a doorway in the rear of the hall a woman, clad in black and wearing a small, frilled white apron, approached Nancy and her friends.

"Good afternoon," Nancy said. "Our car is stalled in your driveway. We should like to have some tea and cinnamon toast, and stay here until the storm is over."

The woman, revealed now as a gaunt, thin-lipped person past middle-age, nodded her head.

"Just take any table," she replied.

"Is there a dressing-room where we could freshen up a bit?" Nancy next asked.

"This is also a hotel, but at present no rooms are taken," the housekeeper said. "Just go into any chamber. There is running water and a dresser with mirror in each."

Nancy thanked the woman and led the way up the old staircase to the upper hall. She opened the door of the first room she came to. The girls found themselves in a plainly furnished bedroom, and proceeded to rearrange their damp and wrinkled clothing and to straighten their hair.

They worked wordlessly and at top speed, eager to be downstairs where there were other persons, for the storm still raged furiously, while the appalling thunder and the blinding blue flare of the lightning made even Nancy feel ill-at-ease. Just as they were completing their toilettes the girls heard an angry masculine voice outside the door.

"Where do you think you are going with that?"

Nancy, always alert to anything savoring of a mystery, turned to her chums with her fingers on her lips.

A girl's voice replied, but Nancy had difficulty in hearing what was said as the storm was so ear-filling.

"—he is one hundred today, so I thought you wouldn't mind—" was all that could be heard.

"That's what *he* says. Let him eat his mush and milk," shouted the man. "Take that tray back! There are three young ladies just in to be fed. Get downstairs and help!"

"But on his hundredth birthday—" the girl's voice came to their ears.

"No back-talk! That's two dollars' worth of food there. Keep out of the tower——"

The sentence was cut short by an ear-splitting crash, followed by the tinkle of falling glass. The girls were blinded for a moment by the glare of the lightning bolt which had shivered an ancient pine tree just outside the house, toppling the hoary evergreen against the building to the destruction of several windows.

The shock of the bolt sent Nancy and her chums reeling against the foot of the bed. After the thunder had died away there followed a death-like stillness. The rain halted abruptly, and from the floor below could be heard the scraping of chairs hurriedly pushed back, together with exclamations of surprise and fright from the guests. Feet thundered on the stairs, as the man who had berated the girl outside the door dashed down to ascertain what damage had been done, and to calm the people.

Then the door of the room in which the three girls were waiting creaked on its hinges and slowly opened inward. Nancy watched it with fascination. Hesitatingly, the slender figure of a girl of about sixteen came into view. She seemed to be dazed and frightened, but whether from fear of the man or of the stroke of lightning Nancy could not guess. Like the woman who had greeted them, the girl was clad in a black dress and a white apron. Clenched in her hands was a tray held stiffly before her. A bouquet of flowers and several dishes of tempting-looking food were in imminent danger of sliding from it to the floor.

"Here, let me take that," Nancy cried, leaping forward.

"Oh! Who——"

The girl gave a faint scream and swayed on

her feet. Nancy seized the tray, and with one motion thrust it into the hands of the amazed Bess.

"We were just in here straightening ourselves out after being caught in the rain," Nancy explained as she put a capable arm about the girl's quivering form.

Regarding the frightened young woman with pity, Nancy led her to the bed and gently pushed her into a sitting position.

"Just rest a minute," she urged. "I think a tree was struck right outside. The danger is past."

The girl sank down obediently; then suddenly leaped to her feet.

"Oh, what am I thinking of?" she cried. "I —I must go. The Twisted Candles——"

CHAPTER II

THE TOWER ROOM

"WELL, what about The Twisted Candles?"
Nancy laughed. "I'm sure you won't lose your
position if you lie down a minute to recover
from your fright. Let me deliver the tray
for you."

The trembling girl relaxed again.

"Who—but I don't know who you are," she
cried, "except that you are very kind and con-
siderate."

"We were just overtaken by the storm and
our car stalled in your driveway," Nancy said.
"You don't have to worry about us at all. We
really are not very hungry."

Outside the rain began again in a steady
downpour, but the thunder had retreated over
the hills, so it was evident that the worst of the
storm had passed. Nancy, however, had forgotten about the storm. Her unfailing instinct
had told her that she was on the threshold of
a mystery.

"My name is Nancy Drew," she told the girl.

"I am Sadie Wipple," the girl replied. "I
—I won't lose my position here, because my

9

foster-parents run the tea room, but I can't sit
here talking, either. I must get to work, or
else——''

"Or else what?" Nancy demanded. "In the
excitement no one will miss you for a few minutes. Go upstairs with your tray."

"I'd like to, but I don't dare," Sadie said,
her eyes widening with fear. "I was forbidden."

"Oh, let's have our tea," George interrupted.
"Is there a mechanic on your staff who can fix
our car, Sadie?"

"I can repair it myself," Nancy said hastily.
"We shall have to wait until the rain stops,
though, no matter who does it. What about
this tray-load of food? It's not improving by
standing here."

"Let us eat it," Bess suggested hopefully.
Good food was Bess's greatest delight, just as
her increasing plumpness was her greatest
worry.

"No, we shan't, Bess," Nancy laughed reprovingly. "There isn't enough to go around,
anyhow. For whom was this tray intended,
Sadie?"

"For Mr. Sidney. He really owns this property, but he lives all alone up in the Tower
Room. He is one hundred years old today, so I
fixed a little spread for him," the girl replied.

Sadie was so pitifully thin, Nancy could not
help but think that the food would do her more

good than it would the man who inhabited the Tower Room.

"I should like to see a man one hundred years old," she said aloud. "And I certainly think he deserves a little party on his birthday."

"Mr. Semitt thinks it is too expensive a trayful," Sadie said. "You see, Mr. Sidney lets my foster-parents have this property in exchange for boarding him and doing his laundry work and so on. I don't know why I'm telling you all this, Miss Drew."

"Listen to me," Nancy said firmly. "I'll pay for the food on the tray, and I'll carry it up and serve it myself. That ought to suit Mr. What's-his-name, I mean your foster-father."

"Oh, would you do that?" Sadie cried, her eyes dancing.

"And what is more, I shall tell Mr. Sidney the spread is your idea," Nancy smiled.

From somewhere below-stairs a voice thundered out: "Sadie! Where are you?"

"Oh, I must go!" the girl cried, and darted from the room in great haste.

"Nancy, you dear old thing," George protested affectionately, putting an arm over her chum's shoulder. "You are always putting yourself out to do a kindness for somebody or other who simply doesn't count in your life at all."

"It's more fun than watching the rain and waiting for toast," Nancy replied. "And I believe this timid girl is much too refined to belong to such a common person. I should like to help her. You girls go on downstairs and I'll meet you there. I must see this centenarian."

"Maybe he is a wizard in an enchanted tower and will cast a spell over you," Bess laughed.

Bess and George went down the stairs in high spirits, while Nancy climbed in the opposite direction, eager for whatever adventure might lie in the Tower Room.

The stairway was unlighted, and the now-distant lightning made queer shadow-play on the walls as Nancy slowly mounted the treads, taking care that nothing on the tray should spill. Except for the growl of far-off thunder and the drumming of the rain there was no sound audible to her from the vast old house.

"A perfect setting for a delightful mystery," Nancy thought. "The biggest problem right now, though, is how I'm going to knock on the door, with both hands balancing a tray!"

She had reached the top of the stairway and stood in front of a heavy, paneled door. A dim light showed beneath it, but no sound came from the other side.

A blank door—but no blanker than the mystery which Nancy, all unknowing, was about to confront. As she stood there some recollection of the seemingly meaningless incidents which had marked the beginning of other adventures flashed through Nancy's mind.

A letter from England, for instance, addressed to Miss Nancy S. Drew, had proved to be for another young lady, informing her that she was an heiress. "Nancy's Mysterious Letter" not only led her into a long chase for another Nancy but, as the volume by that title relates, before the other Miss Drew was found Nancy exposed a crook for whom the United States Secret Service had searched in vain.

Just before that a trip to the country and a halt at a wayside service station had involved Nancy in "The Secret of Red Gate Farm," which she solved at the peril of her life.

No doubt all of us have scores of times rubbed elbows with some refugee from justice, or have figured in some unimportant incident which actually was one link in a long chain of mystery and adventure. Few of us, though, have trained our powers of observation and deduction as Nancy had, although by studying her methods it should not be at all impossible for any intelligent reader to learn them.

Of course, Nancy had an advantage in being so conversant with the professional secrets of Carson Drew, the celebrated criminal lawyer, whose cleverness had just as often saved an innocent person from suffering the penalty of another's crime as it had brought wily lawbreakers to justice. Nancy's mother had died years before; thus, the natural intimacy between father and daughter had deepened wonderfully. Carson Drew's profession had made him well-to-do, although by no means wealthy, so Nancy had her own car, and in this and in other conveyances she had travelled a great deal. In fact, it was in the West that she had uncovered "The Secret at Shadow Ranch."

Ever since Nancy, unaided, solved "The Secret of the Old Clock," which we all recall as the first of her long and growing list of successes, she had worked to educate her faculties. Her reputation was almost as great in River Heights as was her father's, although some of her friends accredited her ability to sheer "luck."

Perhaps it was "luck" that had brought Nancy and her chums to The Twisted Candles; perhaps it was "luck" that had brought her up to the door of the Tower Room, where she stood in the flickering glow of distant lightning.

"I'll just tap at the door with my foot."

Balancing herself against the heavy frame, Nancy tapped at the stout panels with the toe of one dainty, although muddy, slipper. To her surprise, the door swung silently open. Evidently the latch had not been caught fast.

Nancy gazed into one of the strangest looking chambers she—or anyone else, for that matter —had ever seen. The room was a large one, fully twenty feet square, and from all of its walls candles gleamed—candles by the dozen, all winking in the draft of the open door. It was warm in the room, and the heavy air was pungently scented by burning tallow.

Nancy blinked her eyes at the spectacle of the myriad of dancing lights. She entered the room hesitatingly, not certain but that she might trip over a foot-stool or a black cat, or even a trained owl. For it most certainly seemed to be a wizard's den or an alchemist's laboratory which she had entered. In the great arched window directly in front of Nancy burned the massive, curiously twisted candle whose light had beckoned her to the house.

Suddenly, from a low, broad chair before this window, there arose the gaunt figure of a very old man. The candle-light showed to Nancy a picture of Father Time come to life, with his long, silvery white hair sweeping over stooped shoulders, and merging with the snowy beard that spread over his chest to his waist. Shaggy white eyebrows half concealed glowing eyes— strangely youthful eyes—that peered at Nancy from either side of a jutting, hawk-like nose.

"Good evening, Mr. Sidney," Nancy said. "I have brought your dinner. Sadie fixed it up especially for your birthday."

To Nancy's surprise, and to her dismay as well, the aged man stretched forth his bony, trembling arms. In a deep, husky voice that faltered as he spoke, he cried out:

"Jenny—my Jenny, you have come back to me!"

CHAPTER III

"You Are in for Trouble"

Nancy looked at the ancient Asa Sidney with deep perplexity, wondering who Jenny could be.

"I think you are mistaken," she said smiling. "I am Nancy Drew, and this is the first time I have ever been here. Oh—how very queer!"

She set her tray down upon a bench and pointed to a portrait, an oil painting of a golden-haired young woman in the high-waisted, puffed-sleeved style of the eighteen-fifties. The dress was similar in general appearance to the frock Nancy wore, and the girl was quick to realize that in the flickering candle-light she must have appeared to the suddenly awakened old man very much like the portrait come to life.

A tall and artistically tapered candle of opalescent green burned before the painting, its gently-wavering light making the subject of the picture appear to breathe.

"I—I must have been dreaming," old Asa Sidney murmured, dropping his arms and shaking his hoary head. "Well, well," he continued, "that is all we old folks have left. If it were not for our dreams, we should be poor indeed."

Nancy was silent, not certain just what reply, if any, was expected from her.

"However," Asa Sidney said, looking at her with a smile in his eyes, "I think I shall have to get myself some glasses. You were a very pretty vision as you entered the room, and while drowsing here I seemed to see my dear wife step down from the picture up there.

"If I can't tell a very pretty and very much alive young woman from a very old piece of canvas and paint, then I shall have to visit an oculist. Well, one can't expect one's eyes to last much over one hundred years!"

"May I congratulate you on your birthday?"

Asa Sidney laughed a little bitterly.

"Pardon me, my dear," he said, as he resumed his seat. "I am a lonely and soured old hermit. It is of no consequence that this is my birthday. Sadie is a good girl, a very thoughtful young person, to remember a date that means nothing to me and less to anybody else."

"Surely it is worth while to celebrate one's hundredth birthday," Nancy cried. "Why, your name should be in the papers, and your picture, too."

"No, no," protested the old man. "That is all vanity and display. Why should I be honored for an accident? I have not tried to live longer than anyone else. I have read interviews in the newspapers. The reporters always

ask the centenarians how they have lived so
long, and one old codger will say he lived to be
a hundred because he never ate meat, and in
the next county another will say he attributes
his old age to the fact that he never ate anything but meat!

"Ha ha! The only reason one lives to be a
hundred is because one has not died before."

Nancy shuddered a little. Plainly Mr. Sidney was far from happy.

"No, no," the centenarian continued, "very,
very few persons know Asa Sidney is alive at
all, and none of those love the old man except
Sadie, perhaps. She is the only one who ever
visits me for the sake of friendship alone."

"I have two jolly friends downstairs," Nancy
said somewhat shyly, because she did not know
how a plan she had suddenly evolved would be
received. "May we have our tea up here with
you, as a sort of little birthday party? And
perhaps Sadie will join us?"

"Eh? What's that—what did you say your
name was?" Asa asked sharply.

"Nancy Drew," the girl answered, a little
hurt at the strange reception her request had
received. "My father is Carson Drew, the
attorney."

"An attorney, eh? And why did you come to
see me this afternoon?"

"I didn't come to see you at all," Nancy replied, somewhat nettled. "My friends and I

were caught in the storm and stopped here.
Quite by chance I had the opportunity of doing
Sadie a small service in bringing this tray up
to you."

"The tray? Oh, yes indeed! I had quite forgotten about it," Asa said. "Well, well, Nancy,
I do not think I have had a caller for ten years
—although it may have been all my fault.
Bring up your young friends, please do. Tell
Semitt to send up a real spread. Tell him it's
my order. I own the house, so that is quite
all right, you see. He can deduct it from the
rent—ha ha ha!"

All of the old man's conversation only
strengthened Nancy's conviction that she was
in the presence of mystery and drama. She
sped down the stairs to rejoin George and Bess,
and found her chums seated at a table on which
a teapot steamed.

"There you are at last," Bess cried. "I've
almost died sitting here being polite, while all
the time this was teasing me with its perfume."

"This" proved to be a plateful of golden
cinnamon toast from which Bess lifted the
cover.

"Wait a minute," Nancy cried. "Put the
cover back!"

"Wait still another minute? Oh, Nancy,
what did I ever do to you to deserve such
cruelty!" Bess wailed.

"We're going to have supper here," Nancy

announced. "I'll call Hannah, and she can telephone to your folks. That will save us telephone tolls. And we will eat upstairs with the
oldest man any of you ever saw—he is one
hundred years old today!"

George knit her brows.

"Did he invite us?" she asked. "We don't
know him, do we? This is sort of mysterious."

"That's just the reason why Nancy is so en-
thusiastic," Bess laughed. "I think it is a
splendid idea, if we can have a better spread
than cinnamon toast."

She rang the bell industriously, and Sadie
came to answer the summons.

"Sadie," Nancy said, "we are all going to
have our supper with Mr. Sidney. He asked
us. Please tell Mr. Semitt to come here."

Semitt, whose voice the girls had heard in
argument with Sadie, proved to be a tall, rather
heavy-set man, slightly bald as to brow but
wearing long sideburns in the style of English
butlers..

"Yes, Miss?" the manager asked, his voice
purring, his hands clasped, as he bowed to
Nancy.

"We have decided to have a more substantial meal," Nancy said. "Of course, we will
pay for the tea and toast."

Semitt bowed more deeply.

"We shall have some jellied consommé, sliced
breast of chicken, hearts of lettuce with Roque-

fort dressing, nut-bread with sweet butter and mocha layer cake," Nancy recited, mentioning the items that had appeared on Sadie's tray for Mr. Sidney.

"That sounds very good to me!" murmured Bess. "Especially the cake. Is it a three-layered variety?"

Semitt looked at the famished Bess. His pale blue eyes roved over the plump figure, making the girl a bit uneasy.

"I would rather have French dressing on my salad," announced George as she watched the man before her, "and cheese crackers on the side."

"Well, I'll see the Missus," he said slowly. "We like straight orders here. We're not used to having girls come here, telling us how to fix things, but if you——"

He hesitated, and Nancy realized at once it was a question of money which bothered the inn-keeper.

"You shall receive extra pay," declared Nancy firmly, "for your trouble."

This satisfied the man, who bowed and said, "I shall hurry your orders, Miss."

"One thing more," Nancy said. "We want this meal served in the Tower Room with Mr. Sidney, and I should like very much to have you give permission that Sadie join us."

The suave, sleek Semitt bristled. His eyes bulged in his crimson face.

"What is the meaning of this? What do you know of the Tower Room? I—why—who are you?"

"It doesn't matter," Nancy smiled. "We wish to celebrate Mr. Sidney's birthday with him, and he wishes us to dine with him. However, I shall pay well for the supper, as I have promised to pay for the tray Sadie took up to him."

"It will be ten dollars," Semitt announced, his eyes narrowing.

"That's quite all right," Nancy replied, "if the price includes Mr. Sidney's and Sadie's suppers."

Nancy's air of authority cowed the man. He bowed again and left the room, shaking his head and rubbing his hands together.

"I guess he thought I wouldn't pay so much," Nancy laughed as she rummaged through her purse. "Five—and two is seven—eight—can somebody lend me a dollar?"

"Surely," George replied, tossing folded bills across the table. "There're two dollars for my share of the celebration."

"No, you are my guests," Nancy said. "I'll pay this back, George. Now I must telephone to Hannah and tell her that we are going to miss dinner at home.

"Maybe I had better take you up and introduce you to Mr. Sidney first. There is lots of time to call up Hannah later."

As Nancy led her chums toward the stairs Sadie entered the room to clear the table, and Nancy turned back and spoke to her.

"Let Semitt do that," she said. "I'll need your help upstairs—and you are to have supper with us, do you hear?"

"Yes, he told me," Sadie replied timorously. "He wasn't particularly pleased, but he does not wish to offend a patron or lose a big order. Business is not very good."

"I'm glad he thinks I'm a worth while customer," answered Nancy. "I'm sure he didn't at first!"

Bess was counting the tables.

"I guess you do quite a business here," she observed, "when the place is crowded."

"Yes, we do on Sunday nights and holidays, especially," agreed the frail girl.

"It isn't easy work, is it, Sadie?" asked Nancy. "Those heavy trays weigh a good bit, don't they?"

"Oh, yes. Sometimes my arms ache, and always my legs hurt me from standing so much. I really should be taller, I suppose. I have to be on my feet all the time," she added with a tired smile, "and my shoes aren't comfortable to stand in."

There was an air of daintiness and refinement about the young waitress, which was apparent despite Sadie's cheap clothing and menial position.

"Are you allowed to keep the tips that you receive from the generous patrons you wait on?" inquired George somewhat bluntly but nevertheless effectively.

Nancy had been hoping she might learn something of the arrangement that the man Semitt had with this girl but she had not thought it wise to broach the subject on such short acquaintanceship. George felt differently.

Sadie became confused and red. She looked at the floor, and the girls thought they detected a tear on her pale cheek, but she answered bravely:

"I haven't anything, I can't keep anything. They don't think I'm old enough yet to receive pay for my work. But now I better go, or else——"

"I thought you would eat upstairs," pleaded Bess.

"Why, what can be the harm if you have supper with us?" Nancy asked. "I am taking George and Bess up to meet Mr. Sidney, and then I am going to telephone home that I shall be late. I'll help you carry the things upstairs."

"Oh, no! Please don't," Sadie cried.

Nancy led her two chums up the tower stairs, her brow wrinkled in thought. Sadie was evidently unhappy. She was not the Semitts' own daughter. Was it a case of a mistreated adopted child, she puzzled. Then, too, there seemed to be a queer bond between the thin, timid girl and the bearded hermit.

She had arrived at no conclusion when she reached the door of the Tower Room and knocked. Bess and George gave a little start when they saw the hoary and ancient figure whom Nancy greeted.

"I am afraid you will find this strange tower of mine scarcely prepared for your delightful visit," Mr. Sidney said with quaint courtesy. "I rarely have lady callers—about one every ten years is above the average. However, such as they are, my quarters are at your disposal."

Now, for the first time, Nancy had a chance to look about her and survey the room. It was very large, as has been said before, and candles were gleaming everywhere. There was a fireplace on one side of the room, and a broad couch which evidently served the recluse as a bed at night.

Mr. Sidney dragged out a commodious, low rocking chair and arranged black-oak arm chairs of Civil War vintage on either side of it.

"You, my dear," he said with a bow to Nancy, "must take the seat of honor and act as hostess."

"Thank you, but before I sit down I must telephone home," Nancy said. "Sadie is coming to have supper with us. Fortunately it is a cold spread, so your meal will not suffer from your kindness in waiting until ours arrives."

The aged man produced a table elaborately carved in the fashion of a bygone age. With a pocketknife he scratched off driblets of tallow from its surface.

Nancy surmised, that except for the painting of his wife in her youth, Mr. Sidney had no enthusiasm for decoration. The only other objects on the wall were framed texts which seemed to be patent grants from the government. One entire side of the room was taken up with a long work table, a charcoal furnace something like a blacksmith's, together with pots, pans, dye-vats, bars of tallow, beeswax and other similar materials, and row upon row of polished candle molds.

George and Bess were silent, obviously a little frightened at their strange surroundings and the remarkable spectacle the old man made as he moved about the room, scoffing at himself for being slow and clumsy. The candle light made an aura of glowing silver out of his mass of hair.

"Oh, I am forgetting about my telephone call!" Nancy exclaimed. "Please excuse me."

As she felt her way down the dark stairway Nancy heard someone ascending. It was Semitt, grumbling under his breath, and carrying a large, covered tray. A few steps behind came Sadie, similarly burdened.

"Ah, Miss, I'll be ready for you in a moment," Semitt said pleasantly enough.

"I am going to telephone," Nancy explained.

"The booth is at the end of the first hall," Semitt directed.

Nancy had some trouble in establishing the connection with River Heights. Evidently the storm had worked havoc with the lines. At last, however, she heard the voice of Hannah Gruen, the kindly and efficient housekeeper of the Drew household.

"Hello. This is Nancy," the girl explained.

"Praise be! I was sure you had been in a smash-up," Hannah exclaimed. "Where are you now?"

"I don't know exactly where," Nancy replied. "Some place in the country, about twenty miles from home. We took shelter from the storm in the most interesting old tea room. Please do not wait supper for me, Hannah. I will eat here. And Bess and George are staying with me. Will—hello?"

There was a sharp clicking on the wire, and then a long buzzing. Nancy rattled the receiver.

"Hello! Hello! Oh, the line is dead. I have been cut off," she cried. "Hello! Hello!"

"Number, please?" a voice asked languidly.

"I was cut off from River Heights," Nancy explained. "Will you please make the connection?"

"Hold the wire, please."

Nancy's foot tapped the floor impatiently as

the voice was succeeded by a buzz, and the buzz by a series of clicks.

At last she heard Hannah expostulating at the other end.

"—sort of service?" the woman's voice sounded indignantly. "You'd think I was talking to China or the South Pole."

"Hello. Here I am," Nancy interrupted. "Will you call up George's home and Bess's, and explain that I am keeping them out for supper?"

"Yes, but I'll have to tell them where you are," Hannah warned.

"We are eating with an old, old man, a wonderful old man," Nancy explained. "His name is Sidney—Asa Sidney. He is a hun——"

"Asa Sidney? Now you are in for trouble," Hannah almost shouted over the telephone. "Espec——"

Click!

The connection was broken again, and although she tried for five minutes Nancy could not get Hannah on the wire again.

She climbed the stairs, more puzzled than ever. How could Asa Sidney get her into trouble? How did Hannah know about him?

CHAPTER IV

ASA SIDNEY'S STORY

"COME and sit down, my dear! The celebration has already begun," was old Mr. Sidney's greeting as Nancy re-entered the Tower Room.

"I'm sorry to have been so long," Nancy cried, as she took her seat in the big old rocking chair. "The storm must have damaged the telephone lines. I had a hard time keeping a connection."

"My, my!" Mr. Sidney said with a shake of his head. "When I was your age such a thing as talking over wires was unheard of—undreamed of. And now you seem vexed because the miracle does not always perform perfectly."

"Fancy being without a telephone," Nancy cried. "Or without the radio, or automobiles, or airplanes, or electric lights."

"Electric lights? Pooh! I prefer candles," Asa snorted. "Lights out of glass bottles! Bah! But come, this is a party, not a debate. Semitt has made some excellent fruit punch."

"Then I propose a toast to Mr. Sidney, and many happy returns of the day," Nancy cried, lifting her glass high.

With shouts of congratulation the four girls rose to their feet, lifting their glasses to Mr. Sidney, whose beard could not conceal his happy smiles. Then the meal was attacked with gusto, and delicious food it proved to be.

The candlelight sparkled on the silver and china, and in the gayety of the occasion Bess and George lost their awe of the old man, and even Sadie's timidity seemed to vanish. Nancy related how she and her chums had been caught out in the tempest, and how their car had stalled almost at the door of the inn.

"It was the gleam of your candle in the big window there that led us to this delightful place," she said. "I am ready to agree with you, Mr. Sidney, that no electric light bulb could have been as friendly."

"An electric light would probably have gone out in an electrical storm," Mr. Sidney laughed. "No, the old ways are often the best, although I admit in my turn that automobiles are in many ways superior to horses, and certainly the steamboat is far better than sailing ships. Why, I recall——"

The old man's chin drooped as he mused for a moment, a distant look in his dark eyes.

"Yes, it took me seven weeks to make the trip to America," he went on. "Now it is made in less than five days. To think of it!"

"Then you are not an American?" George ventured. "You speak without an accent."

"After eighty-four years in the United States I was bound to change my way of speaking," Mr. Sidney laughed. "I always spoke English. I was born in England, in Liverpool-on-Tyne. When I was nine years old I was apprenticed to a chandler—a man who made candles. There were no free schools then, my dears."

"Was the work hard?" Nancy asked sympathetically.

"For the first year I carried wood and stoked the fires which melted the tallow," Mr. Sidney said. "It was hot work and the hours were long. Then I was promoted to stirring and skimming the hot grease. I was bound out to work until I was twenty-one, at the end of which time I was to receive a suit of clothes, five shillings in silver, and a certificate to prove I was a journeyman chandler.

"It is not boasting to say that I learned very quickly, and when I was fifteen I made my first invention. I invented a candle that was pierced lengthwise by four holes, down which the melted tallow ran instead of spilling over the candlestick. Thus it was saved to be burned when the candle grew shorter. My master made a good profit on that. I received—nothing."

"How unjust!" the girls cried.

"It was, and so I decided to run away. I had only the clothes on my back and no money, but I was determined to go to America," Mr. Sidney explained. "I offered to work my way across, and after many failures the captain of a sailing vessel agreed to give me passage in exchange for labor as a helper in the galley. I washed dishes, served the table, and peeled potatoes," the old man continued.

"For days we would lie becalmed. Our drinking water ran low. It was at the end of the seventh week that we sighted the highlands of New Jersey, and two days later we dropped anchor at Perth Amboy, which in those days was a city as thriving as New York, and was its rival as a port."

"I never even heard of it," Sadie whispered.

"Well, I found work soon enough," Asa went on. "I made candles in Perth Amboy, for although the wealthy used whale oil lamps most of the people still lighted their homes with candles, back in the 'forties. When I had a little money laid aside I moved to Philadelphia, and from there to Pittsburgh. By the time the Civil War broke out I had my own shop at Marietta, on the Ohio River, and was married and a father.

"I did not go to war. I had two children, and I was not called. Evenings I experimented with improvements on candles. Coal oil was coming into use, and I was beginning to turn my mind toward improving the whale oil lamps to burn the new petroleum. I wish I had never, never thought of it."

Again the white head bowed, and a tremor

ran through the old man's body. The girls remained respectfully silent.

"I had invented the twisted candle which brought me fame and fortune. I compounded new waxes and made this candle which burns for eight hours. The secret is in the twist, which makes the candle the equal of one twice as long, if you remember your mathematical axiom that a straight line is the shortest distance between two points. Very well, then a twisted line is the longer. Besides that, the first few inches of the candle are made from very hard wax which does not give so bright a light. The idea was that at dusk, when the candles are lighted, a strong light is not needed. As it grows darker the candle burns down to a softer wax which gives more light.

"It was bought in vast quantities for shops, offices, public halls and such. The Sidney Candle was exported. I leased the patents. Fortune and fame were both mine, and then——"

Again sorrow overcame Asa Sidney, and Nancy leaned forward in her chair, praying that he would continue. Hannah's strange warning still rang in her ears. Would she hear something to explain the meaning of that?

"Ah, men should be content, they should never let success make them greedy," Asa mused.

"Surely a man who is successful owes it to

the world to go on further, to use his talents for the general good," Nancy suggested, hoping to get Mr. Sidney to explain himself.

"It was pride, pride that urged me on, not a desire to better the world," Asa said gloomily. "My two sons were manly little fellows, already in school. Then little Lily came to bless our home. She was the brightest of all the children. She always called herself 'Daddy's partner,' and I let her have the run of the workshop.

"Fool that I was—vain, arrogant fool! If it were not for my conceit Lily would have grown into beautiful womanhood, and my family might be around my chair tonight, proudly celebrating the birthday of Asa Sidney. Instead—tragedy, and years of loneliness——"

The old man's grief was so apparent that Nancy rose from her chair and put her hand on Asa's quivering shoulder.

"I am sorry if we have revived sorrowful memories," she murmured. "Please do not be so sad."

"Sad? I am doomed to be the saddest mortal on earth. Instead of a pleasant home, with grandchildren at my knee, I have lived to see my house divided, feud where there should be affection, envy where there should be love!"

Asa sat up straight and looked about him.

"You must pardon me, my dears, for inflicting a half-century of sorrow upon you. This is no way to repay your kindness. Is there any punch left? Let us drink to the new world of electricity. Salute!"

All drained their glasses of icy fruit punch, Bess looking wistfully at the maraschino cherry which obstinately remained at the bottom of her glass.

"See, the storm has passed and the moon is at my window defying my candle," Asa laughed.

"Oh, and it is late. We must get started!" Nancy cried. "Thank you for entertaining us so royally, Mr. Sidney. May I call again some time?"

"Please come often," Asa answered heartily. "You have taken years off my shoulders. I promise you to let no more ancient sorrows cloud your visits."

And so, with cordial goodbyes and promises to come again, Nancy and her chums bade farewell to Asa and Sadie.

Nancy, obeying an impulse, took Sadie aside and told her again that her father was a lawyer.

"If ever he or I can be of service to you, please let me know," she said.

"I hope to see you again and often," Sadie answered shyly, "even though I cannot imagine myself ever needing legal advice."

"And now for the stalled motor," Nancy called to her chums as they all started down the stairs. "Let me settle the bill with Mr. Semitt, and then I'll see if I can get the engine started."

CHAPTER V

A Strange Complication

"Nancy, if it is mystery you thrive on, you will have your fill discovering the secret sorrow in Mr. Sidney's life," Bess said as Nancy lifted the hood of her car.

"That isn't half of it," Nancy replied, as she jerked the cap off the distributor and began to mop the connections dry. "Look at the spark plugs! They are in perfect wells of water. Throw the flashlight over this way, George."

"Speaking of mysteries," George said, "the insides of an automobile have me baffled. I think you put water in one end and gasoline in the other, but that's as far as my knowledge goes."

"Suppose electricity had never been invented, or gasoline either," Bess suggested. "Maybe Mr. Sidney could have made an automobile to be run by candles!"

"Listen, girls," Nancy interrupted. "When I told Hannah where we were she became very excited."

"Why, is this some sort of notorious den or bandit headquarters?" gasped Bess. "How

thrilling! And you sat there so cool all the
time——!''

''I told Hannah we were supping with Asa
Sidney,'' Nancy continued. ''She gasped and
said something about getting into trouble.
Just then the connection was broken and I
couldn't get her on the wire again.''

''Are you sure you heard correctly?'' George
demanded. ''How in the world could you get
into trouble talking with that kindly old man?''

''I don't know, but I'll find out before the
night is ended,'' Nancy replied. ''Bess dear,
get me a piece of cheese-cloth out of the pocket
in the side of the car, won't you?''

''Here you are. I guessed you would need
it,'' Bess answered, giving Nancy the desired
material. ''It was a thrilling evening, and now
it gets to be real exciting. Wasn't the food
delicious, too?''

''I don't remember tasting it at all, I was so
entranced with Mr. Sidney's story,'' George
confessed. ''And now we are in for trouble as
a result. I can't understand it.''

''At any rate, we won't have any more trouble with the car,'' Nancy said, as she wiped her
hands and lowered the hood. ''All aboard,
ladies. River Heights the next stop.''

''Wait a moment. There is a car turning in
and it may block our path,'' George warned,
as an automobile swerved from the road into
the driveway. The machine almost scraped the

fenders of Nancy's car, and the driver leaned out and asked rather curtly why she was blocking the road.

"Why, it's Great-Uncle Peter!" George exclaimed. "Hello, Uncle Pete!"

"Who—what—George! And Bess, too? Yes, it is. What are you girls doing here?"

The man leaped from his car and strode toward the girls, his face plainly showing anger in the light of the lamps of Nancy's motor.

"We haven't seen you in a long, long time," Bess cried, trying to force a cheery note into her voice. She took hold of the arm of her cousin, as a sort of protective alliance in the advance of the angered man.

Nancy watched the little drama with wonder. She had never heard of Great-Uncle Peter, knowing only that her chums' mothers were sisters who to her knowledge had no brothers or other kinfolk.

"For the second time I ask, will you explain why you two are here?" the man demanded.

"We were just caught out in the storm and stopped here for supper while the rain was— er—raining," George quavered. "This is our chum, Nancy Drew. Our Great-Uncle, Nancy, Mr. Peter Boonton."

Peter Boonton, a man of advanced middle-age, nodded a curt acknowledgment of the introduction.

"Well, run along now," he admonished his

nieces. "It is late for you young girls to be so far from home. And let me warn you that this is scarcely the kind of place your families would care to have you frequent. Goodnight."

He turned on his heel and entered The Twisted Candles Inn.

"Whew," exclaimed George. "What a greeting. Nancy, the plot thickens. And yet if this place is so notorious that we should not be seen here, why does Uncle Peter visit it?"

"Anyhow, I think his advice that we start for home is good," Nancy said. "It would have been better if he hadn't parked his car right in front of mine. I'll have to back out. Oho! Here is another customer!"

To Nancy's chagrin another machine looped into the driveway and drew up close behind her own car.

"This place has become very popular all of a sudden," she frowned, tapping the button of her horn to signal for room in which to back up.

The newcomer did not budge for a moment; then grudgingly he backed his machine and drove it up abreast of Nancy's car. The headlights of his automobile illuminated the car in which "Uncle Peter" had just arrived.

"Say, Miss, do you know who that car belongs to?" the driver asked Nancy.

"Some man," Nancy answered.

"It looks like Pete's," the man said, stepping to the ground and revealing himself to be a person of about the same age as Bess's and George's Great-Uncle.

"Yes, that's Pete's car all right," the man declared emphatically. "See here, you aren't waiting for him by any chance, are you?"

"Certainly not," Nancy answered, gripping Bess's knee as a signal for silence. "We are just leaving, as a matter of fact."

"Don't let me keep you, then," the stranger remarked, absent-mindedly propping one foot on the running-board of Nancy's car and leaning an elbow on the handle of the door. "Now that the old man is past the century mark every relative he has is getting real affectionate. Worrying more about his money than his health, you can bet."

Here was added light on Asa Sidney's strange affairs. Nancy held her breath, hoping that the man would continue his musings aloud.

"Yes, sir! Two generations of fight, and now—hm! Well, Peter Boonton can't put anything over on me," the man muttered. "There'll be a hot scene in the Tower Room tonight or I'm not Jacob Sidney!"

"Oh, are you related to Asa Sidney?" Nancy asked, as the man drew himself erect with a belligerent air.

"Hey? What's that? Do you know Asa?" he cried, thrusting his face into Nancy's car. "Say, who are you?"

"Oh, I just made Mr. Sidney's acquaintance

this afternoon," Nancy replied. "We were caught here in the storm, so we arranged a little party for his hundredth birthday. Sadie helped get it ready and ate with us."

"Sadie! Humph! Asa thinks more of that foundling than of his own flesh and blood," Jacob Sidney snorted.

"He seems to be very lonely," Nancy said suggestively. "He said so himself."

"Oh, he did, did he? And whom has he to blame for that?" the man shouted. "Cutting himself off from everybody and living in an attic making twisted candles all the time. He's crazy, that's what he is.

"You can bet that Jacob Sidney isn't crazy enough, though, to let Pete Boonton fill the old man up with gossip," he added, shaking his fist at the house. "The Sidneys don't inherit any weakness in the head, and a Boonton never got the best of 'em yet!"

With that the stranger dashed into the inn, leaving the girls speechless.

Still silent, Nancy backed the car out of the driveway and headed it for River Heights. Her chums sat silently beside her as the wheels clicked off mile after mile.

Nancy's mind was whirling. Mentally she reviewed the happenings of the afternoon, trying to fit the events together in some sort of pattern.

First, the scolding Semitt had been overheard

giving Sadie. Then the meeting with the old man, and the strange but sorrowful story he had hinted at after the supper shared in the Tower Room. Nancy could not see any connections there.

Hannah's interrupted warning had been meaningless, until the arrival of the two men just as Nancy was ready to leave. Her chums' great-uncle was in some way the rival of Asa's kinsman, Jacob Sidney. Did that innocently involve Bess and George? Was that the "trouble" about which Hannah had tried to warn her, and if so, what trouble could come to Nancy herself?

These problems so occupied Nancy's mind that River Heights was reached before she realized it, and Bess broke the long silence by asking Nancy to leave her at her door.

"It was an exciting afternoon and evening, wasn't it?" she said in farewell. George, who elected to get out with her cousin, added, "Let's plan another visit to Mr. Sidney, no matter what Uncle Peter said."

That plan, however, was destined never to be completed.

CHAPTER VI

HANNAH HAS SOMETHING TO SAY

"HELLO, Dad!" Nancy Drew cried in greeting as she entered her home and saw her parent seated before the fireplace perusing a heavy, leather-bound law book.

"Hello, Nancy! How's the junior partner of Drew and Drew, Inc.?" the famous criminal lawyer laughed.

"A little damp, but otherwise all right," the girl replied, kissing her father warmly.

"I made a little fire to chase out the dampness," Carson Drew said. "Pull up a chair."

"I didn't expect you at home," Nancy said as she settled herself opposite her parent. "Otherwise I would have come straight home for dinner. And yet, if I had, I should have missed what may be the beginning of a real adventure."

"What! Another mystery has you in its meshes?" Carson Drew exclaimed in mock seriousness.

"That reminds me!" Nancy cried. "Hannah! Oh, here she comes!"

"Are you back safe and sound?" the

43

motherly housekeeper demanded. "You run up and take off those damp clothes at once, and take a hot bath before you catch cold!"

"I'm not wet, but thank you for the advice!" Nancy laughed. "I'm just as cozy here as can be. Besides, I must hear the rest of the warning you tried to give me when the telephone connection was broken."

"Warning? What's this?" Mr. Drew cried.

"That's what I want to find out. I was driving with Bess and George and we came to an inn called 'The Twisted Candles,'" Nancy explained hurriedly. "A very, very old man named Asa Sidney lives there and we stayed to help him celebrate his one hundredth birthday. I telephoned to Hannah, and she said, 'Asa Sidney! Now you are in for trouble!' Then the 'phone went dead. What did you mean, Hannah?"

"Well, it's a long story," Hannah Gruen said.

"Then sit down and tell us about it in detail," Mr. Drew urged. "I don't want Nancy to fall into any trouble."

"Oh, it isn't serious trouble, but it may mean a heartache for your daughter, she and those cousins being such good friends and all," Hannah said, seating herself on the extreme edge of the most uncomfortable chair in the room.

"Do go on, Hannah, please," Nancy begged.

"I'll begin at the beginning," Hannah re-

plied. "And I'll tell you how I know all about
it. I got it first hand from Katrina Henkel,
who worked for old Mrs. Sidney until the day
of her death—Mrs. Sidney's, not Katrinka's.
Katrinka went back to the old country a few
years ago, but she and I knew each other real
well because we used to shop at the same
stores."

"Oh, please go on with the story, Hannah.
I'll believe it without all the preface," Nancy
cried.

"Old Asa Sidney," Hannah said primly,
"was responsible for his baby girl's death. He
was a crazy inventor, but that little girl was
the apple of his eye.

"The Sidney family was pretty well off, but
Asa Sidney never stopped fooling with lights.
He was inventing a new sort of lamp, was the
way Katrinka told me. It was a kerosene lamp
that you pumped up."

"That's a new one on me," Carson Drew
murmured. "Are you sure it wasn't a tire, or
a balloon he was inventing?"

"No, it was a lamp," Hannah insisted. "Katrinka told me the idea was to do away with
lamp wicks by forcing the oil up a tube or something like that. It doesn't matter, because it
was never really invented."

"If it wasn't invented—" Nancy began.

"The lamp was only *being* invented, I said.
One night Asa Sidney was working in his lab-

oratory with this poor little child playing around. He had the lamp burning all right, and went to the other side of his workshop for something, leaving the child, when it exploded."

"The child? Or the workshop?" Carson Drew asked, hiding a smile.

"The lamp, Mr. Drew, the lamp," Hannah said a trifle tartly. "It showered the whole place with burning oil and the little girl burned up."

"Oh, how awful!" Nancy cried, clasping her hands. "That explains what made Mr. Sidney so sorrowful. No wonder he can't bear to talk about his early days."

"To go on," Hannah continued, "Mrs. Sidney was away with the two boys for a drive, I think it was. When she came back there was the laboratory in ashes and her baby—dead.

"She didn't say six words to Asa. She left the house that night with her sons. And ever since that day the Boontons and the Sidneys have been at swords' points, the Boontons mad at the Sidneys 'cause Asa let his child be burned up, and the Sidneys mad at the Boontons because Mrs. Sidney left her husband."

"It's still sort of mixed up," Nancy commented. "Who were the Boontons that they should be angry with the Sidneys?"

"Mrs. Sidney was a Boonton before she married Asa," Hannah explained.

"I guessed that, but I wanted to make sure,"

Nancy said. "Now tell me if this is right. Bess Marvin and George Fayne are related to the Boontons, aren't they?"

"Exactly!" Hannah beamed.

"What is the relationship, then?" Nancy asked. "George and Bess didn't seem to know they were related to Asa Sidney at all. Just before we left, though, a man drove up to the place and it proved to be a great-uncle of the girls who scolded them for being there."

"Let me see if I have it right," Hannah said, checking off on her fingers. "Mrs. Sidney went to live with her widower brother, Jeremiah Boonton, with the two boys. One of her sons never married, the other didn't have any children. So Asa has no grandchildren.

"Peter Boonton—he must be Jeremiah's son and Asa's nephew. He had a sister, who is dead now—and her daughters are the mothers of your friends!"

"Let me get this straight," Nancy cried, leaning forward in her earnestness. "Peter Boonton, the man we met tonight, is Asa's nephew. And he is the brother of George's and Bess's grandmother. Then Bess and George are great-grandnieces of old Asa Sidney!"

"That's it!" Hannah cried triumphantly.

"And, of course, being on the Boonton side they are—without knowing it, of course—in the feud against the Sidneys," Nancy exclaimed, sinking back in her chair.

"That's what I meant when I said you were in for trouble taking those girls to have supper with the old man," Hannah said.

"Oh, I hope not. Surely people aren't so silly as to carry a grudge so far. All this tragedy must have happened half a century ago," Nancy protested.

"Well, that isn't all of the story, but I'm not clear about the rest," Hannah said, rising. "There was some sort of reconciliation once between some of the Boontons and some of the Sidneys, and a marriage, I believe, but the feelings were so bitter that both families disowned the couple, or something like that, but it has no bearing on the case."

"Thank you, Hannah, for making everything so clear to me," Nancy said, and as Hannah left the room Nancy told her father the rest of the adventure, including the meeting with Jacob Sidney.

"Well, don't worry. Now you have the missing elements of your story, and the mystery is solved," Carson Drew commented. "It looks as if the old man's money was going to make the feud between the families more bitter, but I am sure it will not affect your friendship with Bess and George, whose mothers seem to have wisely kept them in ignorance of the quarrel. Surely your meeting with the estranged great-granduncle was accidental."

"We had planned to visit him again to-

gether," Nancy said. "Do you think I should
tell the girls of the relationship that their
mothers kept secret or—there's the telephone."

Nancy leaped to her feet to answer the summons of the insistent bell. She was conscious
of the hope that the call would be from Ned
Nickerson, a young man who had chanced to
be of service to her in a previous adventure.
That meeting had developed into a warm friendship, and the preceding Autumn Nancy had
been Ned's guest at the university, where as
star quarterback of the varsity eleven the
young man had made football history.

Oddly enough, the most exciting event was
not the winning touchdown Ned had engineered,
so far as Nancy's interest was concerned, but
the discovery in the stadium of two persons
whom she had long been seeking in the course
of unraveling a mystery and righting a great
injustice, but all that is familiar to those
who shared in reading "Nancy's Mysterious
Letter."

Instead of Ned's cheery baritone, though, the
voice at the other end of the wire proved to be
an unfamiliar feminine one.

"Is this Miss Nancy Drew?" it inquired.

"Yes, this is she," Nancy replied.

"Is this the Miss Drew who was at The
Twisted Candles this afternoon during the
storm?"

Nancy's heart skipped a beat.

"Yes, I was there with two friends," Nancy said. "Who is this, please?"

"This is Sadie Wipple."

"Why, Sadie! I'm so glad to hear from you so soon. I was just telling my father of our meeting, and telling him, too, that I hoped to visit you again soon."

"That is good of you, Miss Drew. I—you—you said your father was a lawyer, didn't you?"

"Yes, but please call me Nancy," was the girl's earnest reply. "I promised that my father would help you if you ever needed advice."

"Thank you, Nancy. I don't need help. Mr. Sidney, though, needs a lawyer, a really good lawyer, Nancy. He asked me please to find one who will come in the morning and make a new will for him," Sadie said.

"I promise you my father will be there," Nancy cried.

A moment later she had exacted the promise from her father, who needed little urging, so interested had he become in the tangled affairs of the Sidney-Boonton families.

"And may I go along?" Nancy asked.

"Hm, this is strictly cut-and-dried legal business," Mr. Drew replied. "Well, we'll see—we'll see!"

CHAPTER VII

ALL IS NOT WELL

To NANCY DREW her father's "We'll see" was as good as outright consent that she should accompany him to the home of Asa Sidney. Carson Drew dearly loved to pretend at being mysterious.

So it happened that bright and early the next morning father and daughter were speeding southward on the county highway, Nancy at the wheel of her snappy little roadster. In a short time they reached The Twisted Candles which proved to be as inviting by daylight as it had been in the gloom of a stormy afternoon.

"That is the Tower Room up there," Nancy pointed out. "And there is Sadie, sweeping the porch."

Sadie looked up as the car swung into the driveway, and dropped her broom. She ran forward to greet Nancy and acknowledged the introduction to Mr. Drew with natural charm.

"Mr. Sidney is expecting you," she said. "You'll show your father the way up, won't you, Miss—I mean, Nancy? I must hurry with my work."

51

"Indeed I will," Nancy said, opening the door. Then she leaned toward Sadie and whispered, "Stay where I can find you. I'll be down in a minute."

Sadie smiled her agreement, and Nancy entered the hallway where Mr. Drew was waiting. She led the way directly upstairs.

"A pretty girl, Sadie," her father said. "But woefully thin to be doing heavy work. She is no advertisement for the food served here."

"Mr. Sidney owns the building and lets Mr. and Mrs. Semitt have it for a tea room and inn," Nancy explained. "They are Sadie's foster-parents. Here we are!"

She rapped at the door of Asa Sidney's Tower Room, and the old man's voice bade them enter.

"Aha, I can't confuse you with a musty old painting this bright morning, my dear," Mr. Sidney smiled. "Mr. Drew, how are you, Sir? Please excuse me for not rising, but I am somewhat weak this morning after a tempestuous night. Won't you draw up a chair?"

"Don't disturb yourself, Mr. Sidney," the lawyer said, placing his bulging brief-case on the table from which the party had supped the night before, and drawing a chair close to the old man's seat.

"I wish to make a new will," Mr. Sidney said simply. "Please understand at the outset that, despite my perhaps dowdy surroundings,

I am prepared to meet your fee. I want the best legal advice, and I can afford to pay for it.''

Nancy stepped quietly from the room and closed the door behind her.

''I know enough about the law business to realize that no third persons are wanted at a time like this,'' she told herself.

It was a sober-minded Nancy who started slowly down the tower stairs. The making of a will was a solemn business, and Nancy could not help thinking that a man who had already passed his hundredth year could not hope to live much longer.

She paused on the first step to glance at the view unfolded through the windows opposite the landing. A corner of an old carriage-shed was visible, and beyond that the edge of a small forest that grew denser and taller as it stretched toward the horizon.

''That must be the woods through which we scooted in the storm last night,'' she mused.

A movement below attracted her attention, and Nancy was immediately alert. She recognized Frank Semitt, Sadie's foster-father, now dressed in overalls. He was carrying a shovel and a large basket which seemed to be extraordinarily heavy.

''Perhaps he has been digging potatoes,'' Nancy thought. ''Yet, if he had been digging something, he'd be coming toward the house, not going away from it. No, he must be going to bury something—and something he doesn't want seen!''

Automatically Nancy's mind deduced the meaning of Semitt's activities, which to an untrained observer would have been dismissed as some unimportant chore.

Semitt paused close to the shed, which Nancy knew from the lay of the land to be at the end of the property farthest from the road. The man looked about him, studied the windows of the house carefully, and then began to dig with speed and fervor.

''That man is up to something dishonest,'' Nancy decided. ''He is trying to hide something.''

The hole satisfied Semitt before it was much more than eighteen inches deep and about as big around. He reached into the basket and took out a box, and Nancy gasped when she saw it. It was unmistakably one which she had seen in Asa Sidney's room the preceding night.

The box was about a foot square and eight or ten inches in depth, made of ebony and strengthened by brass straps and studs of the same material. It had been under one of the chairs Nancy had moved the night before, and she remembered dragging the heavy little box against the wall near the door so no one would trip over it.

At that time she had believed the chest to con-

tain some of the materials with which Asa
Sidney carried on his experiments. Evidently
its contents were far more valuable.

Semitt dropped the box into the hole and
dragged some bleached logs over it from the
woodpile nearby. Then he very carefully
scooped up all the earth dug from the hole,
put it into his basket, and vanished toward
the house with his strange load. It was now all
but impossible to detect that anyone had been
digging near the shed.

"There is more going on at this place than
anyone knows," Nancy said to herself as she
proceeded downstairs. "And unless I am very
much mistaken, Mr. Sidney is the victim of
more than one attempt to get his wealth."

Sadie emerged from a guest chamber on the
second floor, where she had been waiting and
listening for Nancy's descent.

"Hello," she said in a subdued voice.

Nancy sensed that Sadie had something to
tell her, but did not know just how to begin.
So she decided to give the girl an opening.

"Mr. Sidney must have changed his mind
very suddenly about his will," she said.

"Hush!" Sadie whispered, looking cautiously
about. "I did not say anything to Father or
Mother Semitt about it. I—I—oh, Nancy, I'm
so worried and upset. I should not be disloyal
to the Semitts, for after all I owe everything
to them."

"What do you mean, Sadie?" Nancy asked, drawing the girl closer to her.

"Oh, I wish I could get it all straight in my mind," Sadie sighed. "I love old Mr. Sidney. He is so friendless and pathetic.

"Last night, just after you left, a man came to see him. I know him. He is some sort of relative and has been here before, usually late at night. A little while later another man came, who has also visited Mr. Sidney, even oftener than the other caller, although they have never been here together before.

"In a little while the most terrible argument broke out between the two callers. We could hear them shouting, though we were way downstairs in the kitchen. Father Semitt crept upstairs and listened outside the door, I know.

"The arguments would die down and then break out again more violently than ever. After about an hour the second caller left. He caught Father Semitt eavesdropping and scolded him terribly. A few minutes later the other man left, slamming the doors behind him."

"Poor Mr. Sidney! No wonder he said he had had a tempestuous night," Nancy said. "Do you know that the two men are mixed up in a family feud? The first one is related to Mr. Sidney's wife, who left him, and the second is a relative of Mr. Sidney."

"I never heard about that," Sadie said.

"I'll tell you about it in detail when we have a chance," Nancy promised. "Go on with your story."

"Father Semitt was very angry at having been discovered, and when he came downstairs he ordered me to bed," Sadie continued. "I could hear Mr. Sidney pacing the floor, so I went up to see if I could be of any help to him.

"He said to me: 'No, Sadie, the only way you could help me right now would be to summon the best lawyer in the state, and I know you don't know him. Neither do I.'

"So I told him about Mr. Drew, and he asked me to make an appointment with your father. I did it secretly. I am—oh, Nancy, I can't tell you."

"Never mind, then. You must do as you think best," Nancy counseled. "What will Mr. and Mrs. Semitt think of Mr. Sidney's caller, though?"

"Mother Semitt is away for the morning," Sadie explained. "She has walked through the wood-lot to the McIntosh Farm to select some broiler chickens. Father Semitt gave orders he was not to be disturbed. He is working out in the garage, making some repairs on our car."

"Won't Mrs. Semitt be home soon?" Nancy asked.

"Indeed, she is home!"

The two girls shrank back as the harsh voice of Mrs. Semitt fell upon their ears. To Sadie's horror and Nancy's surprise, the inn-keeper's wife emerged from an adjoining room, clad in a spotted dressing gown, her long hair uncoiled and a brush in her hand.

"You had better be more sure of my whereabouts the next time you start blabbing family secrets to strangers, Miss!"

The irate woman thrust her scrawny neck out toward the frightened Sadie, and waved the hair-brush menacingly.

"I heard every word you said, you impudent, deceitful, snippy little foundling brat," the woman screamed. "And as for you, young lady, gossiping with this simple-minded child, I'll settle with you for that this minute!"

CHAPTER VIII

SADIE'S SUSPICIONS

NANCY drew herself erect and leveled her calm blue eyes upon the irate woman. For a moment Emma Semitt faltered.

Then, as if twice angered at allowing herself to be checked by a young girl, the woman burst forth again into a bitter tirade.

"Here we have worked and slaved to make a home for you, an orphan asylum charity child, and this is our reward!" Mrs. Semitt screamed.

Sadie cowered against Nancy, and her thin little body quivered in every fiber.

"If you act like a two-year-old you will have to be treated like one," Mrs. Semitt cried, and with that remark she hit Sadie on the shoulder with the back of the hair-brush.

The girl gave a cry of pain as the brush descended a second time, bruising her knuckles. Nancy's face turned white with mingled disgust, anger and pity for the orphan lass.

"Stop striking this girl," she said in level, cold tones, at the same time pulling Sadie out of her foster-mother's reach and thrusting her behind herself.

"Who are you, to come interfering with a mother correcting a wayward child, I'd like to know?" Emma Semitt fumed. "I never saw the likes of your nerve, you a mere chit yourself!"

"You certainly are proving yourself unfit to take a mother's place," Nancy answered hotly.

"Oh, you—you vixen!"

Choking with rage, Mrs. Semitt lashed out at Nancy, striking her on the chest with the brush. She raised her hand again to repeat the blow, but Nancy deftly caught the woman's wrist and wrenched the hair-brush from her grasp.

"I could have you arrested for that," the girl said, her blue eyes now blazing with a steely glint.

"Yes, maybe you think so! Who do you think you are?" Mrs. Semitt sneered, her courage shaken by Nancy's brave stand. She made no attempt to regain her brush, evidently fearing that Nancy might pay her back in her own coin.

"Who I am makes no difference at all, so far as your attacking me goes," Nancy replied.

"We'll see about that," Mrs. Semitt snarled. "I guess this is my house and I can run it as I see fit, and that includes running out intruders!"

"This is not your house in the first place, and I am not an intruder in the second place," Nancy shot back.

Mrs. Semitt's jaw dropped.

"Wha—what do you mean?" she stammered.

"This house belongs to Asa Sidney and I am here at his invitation," Nancy said.

"Who are you, then, if you know everything?" the woman demanded with respect in her voice.

"My name is Nancy Drew. Carson Drew is my father. Perhaps you have heard of him? He is upstairs with Mr. Sidney now," Nancy explained, a little thrill of triumph in her voice as she saw Mrs. Semitt's arrogance collapse.

"Carson Drew—the lawyer?" Mrs. Semitt asked weakly, feeling for the door frame to brace herself.

"Yes, Carson Drew," Nancy repeated. "The same Carson Drew who smashed the crooked political ring in the county last winter; the same Carson Drew who exposed the fake electric power stock scheme before that."

"I—I know all about him," Mrs. Semitt muttered. "His name is in the papers all the time —and I've seen yours there, too. I didn't know who you were. I'm sorry I hit you. It's my nasty, black temper that gets the best of me. I'm sorry."

"It seems to make a difference to you whom you hit," Nancy could not help observing.

"You won't tell your father, will you?" Mrs. Semitt begged. "I'll do anything to make amends."

"I'll make a bargain with you," Nancy said.

"I will tell Mr. Drew nothing if you will promise not to tell Mr. Semitt anything."

"That's agreed," the woman eagerly cried.

"Very well," Nancy said, turning away and drawing Sadie with her. "If Sadie is subjected to any more punishment, then I shall complain to my father and have him prosecute you."

Nancy walked from the room, with the speechless Sadie in tow. The girl had never before seen Mrs. Semitt bested in an argument; even her husband was afraid of her sharp tongue. Nancy took on even greater proportions in Sadie's estimation.

Mrs. Semitt stared at Nancy's retreating form with angry eyes.

"You had the upper hand this time, young lady," she muttered. "We'll see what happens next time we match wits!"

However, she blanched and almost dropped her hair-brush when Nancy turned on her heel. For a moment Mrs. Semitt thought Nancy had the power to read one's thoughts, but the young woman merely told the housekeeper that she felt hungry after an early breakfast and would have Sadie serve her with cocoa and crackers.

"Yes, yes, that is perfectly all right," Mrs. Semitt said with exaggerated cordiality.

Thus it was that Nancy planned to have further opportunity to consult with Sadie, free from the danger of eavesdroppers. She seated herself in the center of one of the two dining

rooms, and motioned Sadie to sit opposite her
when the girl returned with a pot of chocolate
and a plateful of sweet crackers.

"I promised to tell you about Mr. Sidney and
his quarrelsome relatives," Nancy said.

She told the absorbed Sadie the story Hannah had related the night before, but in less
detail.

"Evidently Mr. Sidney is wealthy," Nancy
concluded. "He made a considerable fortune
when he was younger and he has not spent
much, living in seclusion as he does. So now
the relatives, none of whom took part in the
original quarrel, are trying to get that fortune.
At least, that is the way I figure it out."

"And one side or the other must have succeeded, because Mr. Sidney is making his new
will today," Sadie exclaimed.

"On the other hand, he may be so disgusted
with them all that he is leaving his fortune to
charity," Nancy smiled.

"It would serve the greedy relatives right!"
Sadie replied. "That is——"

A troubled look crossed her face, and Sadie
lapsed into silence, staring into space.

"What is troubling you?" Nancy asked, leaning forward and placing her hand on the sad-
dened girl's shoulder.

"I don't know my own mind," Sadie answered with a catch in her voice. "Oh, Nancy,
I wish I were as smart as you are. Everything

seems so clear to you, while to me it is all a muddle.''

"Nonsense," scoffed Nancy. "Come, maybe I can help you!"

"I am an orphan—I guess you know that from the way Mother Semitt talked," Sadie said rather bitterly. "I know nothing about my parents. I was left in a church when I was a tot, and the Semitts took me from an orphan asylum when I was six years old. I have worked hard for them. When I went to school I came home to find dozens and dozens of dishes piled up for me to wash. I think I owe the Semitts nothing. I have paid my way.

"Only Mr. Sidney was nice to me. The Semitts were always sweet and kind to me, too, when he was around. I am sure I owe him more loyalty than I do my foster-parents. And yet——"

"What is the matter, Sadie? Do you suspect that the Semitts are not being honest with Mr. Sidney?" Nancy asked gently.

"Why, how did you guess?" Sadie cried. "Do you also suspect them?"

"Yes, I do, and with good reason," Nancy said. "However, it is only a suspicion."

Her mind flashed to the box she had seen Semitt burying. Wisely she resolved that, much as she pitied Sadie, it would be better to hold her own counsel for the time being.

Sadie, though, warmed by the new friendship,

leaned toward Nancy, her eyes round with excitement.

"I am pretty sure that Father Semitt is robbing Mr. Sidney, while the old man's mind is taken up with his quarrelsome relatives," she whispered. "I have seen him sneaking around mysteriously, and sometimes he suddenly seems to have a lot of money, much more than this unknown wayside inn ever earns. Of course, I——"

"That is very interesting," Nancy said loudly. "Once we had some baby robins in a vine outside a bedroom window, too. Do you have many wrens?"

Sadie's mouth opened wide in astonishment. Had Nancy suddenly lost her mind?

CHAPTER IX

THE BURIED BOX

"Good morning, Miss! We don't often have patrons as early as this."

Sadie gulped. The voice was that of Frank Semitt, and at once she understood why Nancy had suddenly interrupted her conversation with the strange remark about birds.

"Have you been served well?" Semitt asked, approaching the table. "Sadie, get up ·and fetch the young lady a glass of water!"

"Oh, please don't bother," Nancy smiled, restraining Sadie. "I was just eating to pass the time away."

"Well, it's as good a way as any to pass time," Semitt observed, "providing you can pay for it. And also, if you don't care about how fat you get, either."

He laughed at his dull joke, and with an appraising glance at the pretty girl in her modish frock, Semitt pulled a chair from an adjoining table and prepared to monopolize the conversation.

"You live hereabouts?" he asked Nancy. "Or are you touring? I don't remember seeing you before, but I sure hope it won't be the last time.''

''Oh, I have seen you before, Mr. Semitt, and I have heard about you, too,'' Nancy said sweetly.

The inn-keeper preened himself.

''Who told you about me?'' he asked, a foolish grin on his characterless face.

''Why, I was here last night, don't you recall?'' Nancy smiled. ''I arranged the little dinner party up in the Tower Room.''

''Suffering cats!'' exclaimed Semitt. ''I—you—but hold on, you didn't spend the night here, did you?''

''No, I came back this morning with my father, whom Mr. Sidney wished to consult.''

''Oh, are you Dr. Crosby's daughter?'' Semitt asked. ''I knew he had quite a young lady in his family, but I didn't dream she'd be so good to look at. Doc Crosby—begging your pardon—isn't any too handsome himself.''

''I don't know Dr. Crosby,'' Nancy said. ''My father is Carson Drew.''

Frank Semitt's face turned a shade paler, and he swallowed heavily two or three times.

''Car-Carson Dud-dud-Drew — he's upstairs?'' he gulped.

''Yes, he has been there for over an hour now,'' Nancy replied coolly. ''It must be an important consultation.''

''Oh, I'm sure it can't be—I mean yes, it

must be," Semitt stammered, rising hurriedly.
"Er—excuse me a minute. I have to mass the
grow—I mean, maw the gross, you know. Mow
the grass. Ha ha! There's no charge for your
snack, you understand. We like to cuss our
treatamores—I mean, treat our customers——"

The agitated man fled from the room, Nancy
watching his retreat with amusement.

"Does he suffer from some nervous ailment
or other, Sadie?" she asked.

"I never saw him so upset," the wondering
girl replied. "He seems to be afraid of your
father."

"Which seems to confirm your suspicions,"
Nancy remarked. "I think I shall keep an eye
on Mr. Semitt."

"Oh, dear, if only I knew who my rightful
parents were," Sadie sighed. "It would give
me courage to leave this place and make my
own way."

"Perhaps my father can help you trace your
parents," Nancy suggested. "There must be
a record of your birth somewhere. I shall ask
him to have some clerk in his office start a
search."

"Oh, Nancy, would you do that?" Sadie exclaimed, clasping her hands as her eyes filled
with grateful tears. "I know I will never be
able to pay you back, or to pay your father all
at once, but I shall work and save and pay him
his fee a little at a time."

"Nonsense," scoffed Nancy. "Dad has plenty of money, and a heart of gold! He wouldn't charge you a cent."

"If only you could realize what it means not to know who you are," Sadie sighed. "The Semitts keep reminding me constantly that I am a waif who might have met any fate but for their generosity."

"Don't worry. If it is at all possible to establish your identity it will be done," Nancy said soothingly. "Why, here comes Dad now. I know his step."

She arose and entered the hall, meeting her parent at the foot of the stairs.

"Are you ready to go now?" she asked.

"No," Mr. Drew replied. "This is a strange and complicated state of affairs Mr. Sidney's case has involved me in. After what I have heard I shall not leave the house until the document is witnessed by someone competent to stand up under a gruelling in court.

"I want you to help me, Nancy. Speed is essential. Will you go to the Smith's Ferry branch of the State Trust Company and ask for Mr. Hill—Raymond Hill? He is the executive vice-president of the company in charge of that branch of the bank.

"Tell Mr. Hill I want him to witness an important document, and bring him back with you. I'm well acquainted with him, and he knows me well enough to grant me this wish.

Do you know the way? Can you remember the name?"

"Yes, indeed!" Nancy replied, thrilled at the opportunity to help her distinguished father complete an important commission, and excited further by the new element of mystery.

Nancy ran back to the table and told Sadie that she had to go on an important errand for her father, but that she would return shortly.

As she spoke, Nancy saw the swinging door leading into the kitchen move slightly.

"I think I'll go out this way, it's shorter," she said, skipping across to the door and suddenly pushing it ajar. As she had expected, the portal did not open far, and there was a muttered exclamation from behind it.

"Oh, I'm so sorry! Did I hit somebody?" Nancy asked, and then Mrs. Semitt was revealed, looking rather dazed and rubbing her ear.

"No, not at all," Mrs. Semitt said.

She wheeled about, darted through the kitchen, and vanished into the garden. Nancy was at her heels, but Mr. Drew's voice called her back.

"You were a little too fast for me," he smiled. "I just wanted to tell you that Peter Boonton and Jacob Sidney are due here this morning. We want the will signed and witnessed before they arrive. That is the reason for the speed."

Sadie listened with awe to the famous man, wishing in her heart that when the identity of her father was learned it would reveal him as a person to be proud of, too, although she feared that anyone who would abandon his daughter must be a scoundrel.

Nancy nodded her understanding to Mr. Drew and left the house. She saw Semitt violently cranking his automobile, the battery of which had evidently been allowed to run down through carelessness, because the car was a new one of fairly expensive make. Mrs. Semitt was beside him, talking and gesticulating violently.

"Speed is necessary in my errand," Nancy thought to herself. "On the other hand, I may never again have an opportunity like this one to look at that buried box."

She located the shed she had seen from the tower window and sped toward it. It was no task at all to roll the logs in the improvised woodpile, and to uncover what Semitt had concealed there.

The box was heavy, but anxiety gave Nancy added strength. She saw at a glance that a yellowed sheet of paper pasted on the lid bore the inscription:

"Private Property of Asa Sidney."

CHAPTER X

A Race against Time

HUGGING the heavy ebony-and-brass chest close, Nancy ran around the far corner of the house and jumped into her car. A push on the starter made the sturdy motor roar into life. Shifting silently and smoothly, Nancy was already up to a speed of thirty miles an hour as the machine left the exit of The Twisted Candles.

The highway was clear, and Nancy darted a glance at her rear-vision mirror to see if anyone were on the road behind. What she saw reflected there caused her to shove the accelerator button to the floor. Frank Semitt's big car had lurched into the road and was roaring after her!

"Does he know where I am going, and why?"

Semitt's car, although left behind by Nancy's first rush, began to crawl up. Past the sixty-miles-an-hour mark swept Nancy's powerful little roadster, but Semitt's car seemed fully as fast.

"There's no doubt about it. He is after me," Nancy told herself. "Either he is going

to try to prevent me from bringing Mr. Hill
back or else he saw me with his stolen box.''

Smith's Ferry was a small community about
halfway back to River Heights, but on a diag-
onal road; a road for which Nancy kept watch
eagerly. Soon she detected certain landmarks
which told her it was not far ahead, and with
that a strategic plan flashed into her agile
brain.

She allowed her speed to slacken a little, until
Semitt's car was less than fifty feet behind.
Then she leaped forward again, playing a tan-
talizing game of tag with the inn-keeper.

To further her plan, Nancy dared look back
over her shoulder a second. The fleeting glance
disclosed Sadie's foster-father crouching over
the wheel of his car, his teeth clenched, his face
purple.

Nancy, calculating her speed and the road
with nice precision, almost passed the Smith's
Ferry highway; then, with a twist of her wheel
she shot into the fork. The snappy little roadster teetered on two wheels as it made the
sharp curve at high speed.

Crash!

Nancy slowed down to glance behind her. A
look of relief passed over her pretty face, and
then she urged her car forward again.

Semitt, in his blind rage, had fallen into the
trap. So intent had he been upon passing
Nancy's car that her abrupt turn had caught

him unaware, and he had shot forward on the road to River Heights. As he had jammed on his brakes, his speeding car had skidded in the gravel and had left the road, crashing through a barb-wire fence.

Two minutes later Nancy was traversing the main street of Smith's Ferry at a sedate pace. She found the bank without difficulty, parked her machine, picked up the precious ebony box and entered the financial institution without a hair being out of place or a pleat wrinkled. Only her crimsoned cheeks and dancing eyes gave any evidence of the excitement through which she had just gone.

"I should like to speak with Mr. Hill—Mr. Raymond Hill," Nancy told the teller.

"Have you an appointment?"

"No, but if you will tell him I am from Mr. Carson Drew on important business I am sure he will see me," Nancy replied.

The teller smiled, as if amused at the assertion that so young a girl could make important bankers violate rules for any business in which she was concerned. However, there was respect in the clerk's voice when he returned and said that Mr. Hill would see Nancy at once. He proved to be a man of Carson Drew's age, although less muscular and active looking.

"What can I do for your father?" he asked Nancy. "Oh, don't be surprised. I am no detective, but I have often seen your picture on your father's desk in his office, so I know you are his daughter.''

"My father wants you to witness an important document over which there may be some legal trouble," Nancy said directly. "My car is outside and I will drive you to the place. It is a matter in which minutes are precious, Mr. Hill."

"Then I shall come at once," the banker hastened to reply, jumping up from behind his desk and donning a hat he snatched from a rack.

"First, though, I should like to rent a safety deposit vault for this box," Nancy said. "Or, if you will deposit it in your safe, that will be just as well."

"That shall be done at once," Mr. Hill said, pressing a button.

"Of course, I should like a receipt," Nancy added.

"You are a cautious young business woman," the banker chuckled.

A man in the uniform of a special policeman entered the room in response to the summons, and Mr. Hill gave him the precious box with instructions to place it in the gold vault.

"You write your own receipt," he told Nancy. She seized pen and ink, wrote a brief but accurate description of the box, and Mr. Hill signed the paper.

"Now, let us be on our way," he said.

Nancy escorted the banker to her car, and in less than a minute headed it back toward The Sign of the Twisted Candles. Mr. Hill leaned back in the seat without speaking, although his eyes traveled nervously to the speedometer from time to time.

Just as the end of the road came into view, an automobile darted into it, and as Nancy swept by, she saw from the corner of her eye that it was Semitt's. A second glance in the mirror showed the inn-keeper standing up, shaking both fists over his head at the retreating machine.

A few minutes later Nancy swerved into the driveway of the old mansion, and brought her car to an easy halt at the steps of The Twisted Candles.

"I'm not being kidnaped, am I?" Mr. Hill joked, as he stepped out of the machine. "What is this place, and where is Mr. Drew?"

As if in answer to his question the lawyer stepped out onto the piazza and greeted the banker.

"You made excellent time," he said to Nancy. "I scarcely expected you to have reached Smith's Ferry yet. None of the interference we have feared has made its appearance as yet."

Mr. Hill followed Mr. Drew into the house, and Nancy sat down on the steps to allow her tense nerves and muscles to relax. Her mind,

however, did not relax. She wondered what
Semitt would say to her when they met again,
for they inevitably would have to meet. She
wondered, too, at the contents of the box, and
at the crisis in the affairs of Mr. Sidney that
made her father so concerned.

"I wonder if it affects Sadie in any way?"
Nancy pondered. "Wouldn't it be splendid if
Mr. Sidney were to leave her some money in
his will? Perhaps he will bequeath her the
house, and then she will be the owner of The
Twisted Candles, and the Semitts will be her
employees!"

The idea pleased Nancy. She wished there
was some way in which to put the thought into
Asa Sidney's mind before his will was signed
and sealed.

"Perhaps if I put my mind to it the thought
will come to Mr. Sidney now," Nancy mused.

However, that very important idea was
driven from Nancy's mind at the sight of an
automobile speeding along the road toward
the inn.

"Here comes Semitt," she said to herself.
"Now for the show-down."

It was not Semitt's car, however, that
skidded to a halt in front of the tea room, nor
was he in the second car which arrived a moment afterward from the opposite direction.
However, when Nancy realized who the arri-
vals were, she felt her heart skip a beat.

CHAPTER XI

A Reunion in the Tower

From the first car leaped Jacob Sidney. Looking neither to right nor to left he sprinted for the porch. Peter Boonton jumped from the second machine, and likewise dashed for the piazza steps where Nancy was sitting.

The girl was no slower than either of the men. She leaped to her feet and pretended to stumble, leaning against the door for support. Boonton and his estranged cousin, panting heavily, drew up side by side in front of her.

"Stand aside and see that no one follows me," Jacob Sidney commanded.

"Let me in! I am in a hurry to see Mr. Sidney on a confidential matter," Boonton puffed.

"He is busy just now," Nancy said. "He is in conference and does not wish to be disturbed. Won't you sit down?"

"With whom is he conferring?" Boonton cried.

"I am not at liberty to discuss that," Nancy replied sweetly. "Won't you two gentlemen have some iced tea?"

"Two gentlemen?" Jacob Sidney sneered. "I can account for only one here."

"Thank you for the compliment, Sidney," Boonton retorted. "I am glad you admit you are no gentleman."

"Don't speak to me, you—you weasel, you!" Sidney fumed. "I'll have you understand that you and I are not on speaking terms!"

"I'll bring you both pencil and paper," Nancy suggested, still not budging from the door. "You might write each other notes if you won't talk."

"Say, who are you, anyhow?" Boonton demanded.

"Why, Mr. Boonton, we were introduced last night," Nancy replied. "Bess and George were here with me, don't you remember?"

"You won't be here with Bess and George again, here nor anywhere else," Boonton roared.

"I remember you now," Sidney exclaimed. "You were sitting in a car right out there in the driveway. Say, what is your business around here?"

"I am a chauffeur," Nancy said. "Or is a lady chauffeur a chauffess? What would you say, Mr. Boonton?"

"Why, I would say a chauffeuress," Boonton replied.

"No, the French way would be 'chauffeuse'," Sidney interjected. "It is a French word."

"Really?" Nancy asked, wide-eyed. "Isn't that odd? What does it mean?"

"Why, it means—see here!" Sidney yelled, stamping his foot. "You are just trying to keep me with your fool questions from going upstairs! I can see through your tricks!"

Nancy heard a commotion in the hall behind her, and wondered for a moment if she were to be attacked from the rear as well. The clanking and swishing soon stopped, however, and she once more turned her attention to the two men who were now in violent debate.

"I'll go up first because I'm his blood relative, and bear his name," Sidney shouted.

"I have as much right to see him as you have," Boonton argued.

"I was here first," Sidney snapped.

"I got to the door ahead of you, didn't I, Miss?" Boonton appealed to Nancy.

"Why don't you toss for it?" Nancy suggested. "Has either of you a quarter?"

Boonton started to dig into his trouser-pocket for a coin, when Sidney suddenly pushed Nancy aside and jerked open the door. With a strangled cry Boonton caught his cousin by the coat and the two men leaped into the hallway together, Nancy at their heels.

A new obstacle confronted them, however, and Nancy felt like giving three cheers to Sadie, who had acted with quick-wittedness to help the situation. Across the bottom steps of the stairs

she had stretched a broom and a mop. Many
of the treads were dripping soapy water, and
halfway up knelt Sadie, surrounded by three
buckets of water. She was swinging a scrub-
bing brush.

"Hey! Let us up!" Boonton shouted.

Sadie gave a start and upset one pail. The
men leaped to one side just as a cascade of
dirty water splashed down upon the spot where
they had been standing.

"Oh, you scared me!" Sadie cried. "Wait,
and I'll mop the water so you can come up
without slipping."

While the two fortune-hunters fairly danced
with impatience Sadie carried down one pail
of water, then climbed the stairs again and
carried another to the top. Then slowly she
wiped away the excess water.

Her skirts were soaked and her hands were
red, but for all that Sadie seemed to be enjoy-
ing herself. She picked up the broom and the
mop, and then the two men made a rush for the
stairs.

Of course they jammed together, clawing at
each other for a moment. Nancy and Sadie,
their arms entwined, could not avoid the gales
of laughter which the absurd battle provoked
in them. At last Boonton gained the advantage
and darted upward, Sidney only a step behind.

"That was splendid work, Sadie, splendid!"
Nancy whispered. "It gave Mr. Sidney and

Dad another five minutes of precious time. That was a real stroke of genius, getting those pails and mops and then upsetting the water.''

Sadie glowed with pride at the praise. She was not accustomed to it, and the words left her blushing and speechless.

With a parting pat on the back Nancy left Sadie and darted upstairs after the two men. She caught up with them just as they burst into the door of the Tower Room.

"In the name of the law I demand that you stop!" Peter Boonton shouted as he threw open the door.

"Don't pay any attention to him!" Jacob Sidney yelled. "But stop whatever you are doing!"

Nancy saw Asa Sidney leaning back in his favorite chair near the great, ever-burning twisted candle. Standing at a small nearby table, with his back turned, but staring calmly over his shoulder at the intruders, was her father, Carson Drew. At the table, with pen in hand, as if he had just finished writing, Raymond Hill was seated. A number of sheets of paper, covered with writing, were in view.

"What branch of the law do you represent?" Mr. Drew asked Boonton quietly, gathering up the papers and folding them lengthwise. "Are you a policeman, a sheriff, a marshal, or a constable?" he continued. "Speak up!"

Nonplussed, Boonton stood stock still, his

mouth opening and closing like a goldfish's.

"I—I'm not an officer," he said finally. "But hasn't a relative any rights in a case like this?"

"A case like what?" Mr. Drew asked. "I have just finished drawing up Mr. Sidney's will, which Mr. Hill, here, has witnessed. Is there anything illegal about that?"

"I demand to see the document," Jacob Sidney announced, striding forward. "I suspect that you have put some ideas into my kinsman's head."

That remark angered Nancy, for she knew her father's code of justice was rigid and unyielding. Her blue eyes flashing, she strode forward and faced the speaker.

"I resent that remark, Mr. Sidney," she cried with a toss of her blond head. "This is the first time my father has seen Mr. Sidney, and before last night he did not even know of his existence. I demand that you apologize!"

Boonton and Sidney retreated a step before the girl's onslaught.

"I—you—who are you, anyhow?" Jacob asked uncertainly. "Everybody seems to be running this show except those who are most interested."

With a deep-throated chuckle Asa Sidney arose from his chair and entered the circle of disputants.

"It is more than passing strange," he said in his quaint, old-fashioned stilted English, "that

I should have been left alone and unprotected all these years, and now suddenly you become so deeply concerned over me and so worried about my affairs. I assure you, my nephews, that I am just as able to care for myself today as I was a year ago."

"I don't doubt it, Uncle Asa," Jacob said in mollifying tones. "I not only think you are able to care for yourself but you are the first person I should wish to consult in any transaction. I just want to warn you against putting too much confidence in utter strangers."

"And not only utter strangers, but scheming relatives," Peter Boonton interjected. "You know I have only your best interests at heart."

"Just the same, a stranger may prove to be a great friend," Nancy murmured.

Asa overheard her remark and burst out into a chuckle. He clapped Nancy on the shoulder, finally letting his arm rest there affectionately.

"You should take your daughter into partnership, Mr. Drew," he said. "I think she would be an asset to any firm."

"She is my silent partner," the lawyer smiled. "Yet a most active one. I frequently consult Nancy, and her advice is always good."

"She reminds me very much of my Jenny," Asa said sadly. "That makes me even more fond of her."

Boonton and Jacob Sidney listened to this conversation with deepening frowns.

"I hope, Uncle Asa, that you are not permitting a chance likeness to unduly influence you," Jacob said.

"When I need your advice I shall consult you," Asa said rather testily. "And I faintly suspect that I shall live another hundred years before that becomes necessary."

"I was only trying to help you," Jacob muttered.

"Oh, do you really wish to be of service to me?" Asa asked, a twinkle appearing in his eyes.

"Yes indeed," Jacob replied eagerly, eager to ingratiate himself with the old man.

"Let me do it," Peter shouted, thrusting himself forward. Nancy could not help likening the actions of the men to those of scheming little boys, although each was almost old enough to be her grandfather.

"Well, you may both do it," Asa said, stroking his long beard judiciously.

"What shall we do?" chorused the nephews.

"Get out!" Asa thundered in a tone that surprised everyone. "Get out of here and stay out until I ask you to come back! You have sickened me, both of you. You think I have money, and are fluttering around like a pair of vultures waiting for me to die! Go!"

Peter and Jacob paled at being shown up like this before the lawyer, the banker and, most of all, before a mere slip of a girl.

Nancy felt Asa's hand tremble as it rested on her shoulder, and the old man's breath wheezed in his throat. He swayed on his feet and clung for a moment to the girl's arm to steady himself.

The two grasping nephews backed slowly toward the door. Nancy feared that another outburst from old Asa would seriously sap his feeble strength, so she slipped toward the door to speed the departure of Peter and Jacob.

Those two worthies, however, had grown desperate at the thought of losing the inheritance. Normally, both were respectable and respected men, honest and industrious. Yet visions of an unearned fortune had somehow appealed to their baser natures; they were not going to let it slip by them without a struggle.

"Please be calm and reasonable," Peter began in a low, soothing tone. "I was impetuous and I beg you to bear me no ill-will, Uncle."

Asa wearily signaled to Nancy to open the door. She grasped the knob and swung the portal wide.

"Oh! I—I dropped something. I—I—I——"

There, blushing and stuttering, revealed for everyone to see in his chagrin, crouched Frank Semitt on the doorstep. He had had his ear to the keyhole. He had been eavesdropping!

CHAPTER XII

SCHEMES AND SANDWICHES

"WHAT are you doing here?" Nancy snapped, pointing an accusing finger at Semitt.

Crouching on his heels like a great, pale frog, the inn-keeper stared at the girl in dismay.

"I—I dropped something," he stammered. "I was just looking for it."

"How did it happen that it was dropped so close to the door?" Nancy demanded.

Semitt quailed before Nancy and took a hop backward.

"It—I—when I was cleaning this morning— I dropped a dime," he spluttered.

"Are you sure you didn't drop it when you stopped so quickly in the road you skidded into a fence?" Nancy demanded, repressing a smile.

"Maybe I did—I mean certainly not!" Semitt squeaked, taking another step backward as Nancy shook her finger again.

"You were eavesdropping, as a matter of fact," the girl accused, advancing toward the inn-keeper, while the five men crowded into the doorway to watch the amusing but dramatic spectacle.

"Never!" Semitt wailed. "I wouldn't do such a thing."

"Why did you pursue me this morning?" Nancy cried, taking a fresh tack.

"I didn't—" Semitt cried, hopping back once again at the new accusation. He teetered for a moment on the top step, and then with a yell of fright toppled over and fell headlong down the stairs.

He picked himself up on the landing, after completing a somersault and a half with no visible damage except that to his pride.

"Are—are you hurt?" Nancy gasped.

"I'll sue you for pushing me down!" Semitt shouted, rubbing his head and one shin. "I might have broken my neck!"

"Frank," Asa called down to the bruised and outraged inn-keeper, "oh Frank, when you get all the way down, will you open the front door for these two gentlemen? They are coming right after you—but right side up, I hope."

Peter and Jacob looked startled; then, as if realizing they would only hurt their cause by staying longer, they silently and sheepishly descended the stairs behind the limping Semitt.

Asa sighed deeply as the men vanished, and reached for the doorframe to support himself. Evidently the strain of the morning's events had shaken him deeply.

Nancy flew to his side and led the aged man back to his favorite seat, where she settled him comfortably, a pillow at the back of his head and a stool at his feet.

"A remarkable adventure, Carson," Mr. Hill said to Mr. Drew. "I did not expect so much drama and comedy to attend the signing of a will, and I am grateful to you and to Nancy for allowing me to share in the events."

"Somehow, excitement always seems to follow my daughter around," the lawyer laughed. "I really think she is a magnet for adventure."

Nancy smiled at the men.

"If that is true I ought to be locked up some place," she laughed. "I'd hate to think myself responsible for all that happened here today."

"You were certainly responsible for that man Frank's unusual descent of the stairs," Mr. Hill laughed back. "And now, I think I shall return to my business. I'll certainly remember all that you told me, Carson, at our little conference. Was there anything further?"

"No, I am sure you understand the general situation as well as I do," Mr. Drew replied. "Shall Nancy drive you back to the bank?"

"No, no!" Mr. Hill protested. "I shall call up my chauffeur who is no doubt waiting at the bank for me, and have him come here. It must be very close to luncheon time."

"I don't have to consult my watch to agree with you," Carson Drew smiled. "I feel hungry. How about you, Nancy?"

"I had some cocoa and crackers a little while

ago,'' Nancy replied. ''But I could eat—indeed I could! And I can wait, too.''

''Good! I want to examine that man Semitt,'' her father said. ''Well, then, goodbye for the present, Raymond.''

Mr. Hill left the room, and Mr. Drew paused in the doorway for another word with old Mr. Sidney. A soft footfall was heard on the steps and Sadie appeared, carrying a loaded tray.

''I—I made some sandwiches,'' she said shyly. ''And a pitcher of iced tea with fresh mint in it.''

''Wonderful! Wonderful!'' the lawyer exclaimed heartily. ''And you must sit right down with us and share the meal, Sadie. I should like to become much better acquainted with you.''

''Sadie is a very good girl, my only comfort and helper,'' Asa said, lifting his head from the pillows. ''My dear child, sit here beside me. You look very tired.''

''I'm not at all tired,'' the young waitress replied stoutly, putting the tray on the table and lifting the cloth that covered it. ''Now, what shall I give you, Mr. Drew? I made both kinds of sandwiches—dainty ones and good, thick, substantial ones.''

''What a picture they make, too,'' Mr. Drew commented. ''You are an artist, Sadie, an artist who uses foodstuffs instead of paints and a tray instead of a canvas.''

A squat jug, bedewed with moisture, ice clinking against its sides and a bunch of fragrant mint projecting above its rim, stood in the center of the tray. Glasses, with a little pile of plates and napkins flanked the pitcher. There were platters heaped high with three-cornered sandwiches of white, brown and rye bread. A few nasturtium blossoms had been scattered on the tray as a final touch.

"There are chicken sandwiches, cucumber-and-mayonnaise sandwiches, and egg salad on the white bread," Sadie pointed out. "The brown bread has crabapple jelly and chopped dates with walnuts. The rye bread has ham and Swiss cheese with mustard. Please help yourselves."

No one needed a second invitation. Mr. Sidney proved that the exciting events had not robbed him of his appetite, and the others of course had had theirs whetted the more by the dramatic adventures of the morning.

After his fifth sandwich and third glass of iced minted tea, Mr. Drew announced that he was going to "have a word with Semitt," and excused himself.

"Don't be harsh with Frank," Asa requested. "He is not a bad fellow at all, just too curious over matters that do not concern him. At that he might be excused for trying to learn what all the hubbub was about."

"I have no legal authority to be harsh with

him, or to force him in any way," Mr. Drew replied. "If he will volunteer any information in reply to some questions, well and good. If he does not, no matter."

"After all, he is Sadie's foster-father and I am indebted to him for that," Asa said. "Sadie, that was a delicious lunch. Things always taste much better when you prepare them. Even if Frank brings my tray of mush and milk I can tell whether or not you prepared it."

"Oh, Mr. Sidney, you are just having fun with me," the orphan returned, coloring at the compliments. She arose to clear up the remains of the meal as Mr. Drew left the room.

"Just sit quietly for a while, Sadie. There is no hurry," Asa said. "It is very pleasant, having such charming callers as Nancy and yourself. Tell me something interesting. What is going on in the world?"

"The transcontinental air mail is making daily stops at River Heights now," Nancy ventured, wondering what gossip would please the old man.

"Remarkable, remarkable," Asa mused. "When I came to this country it was a month's journey here from New York. Now I suppose one can fly from New York to San Francisco in a few days."

"In one day, Mr. Sidney," Nancy said.

"Well, well, can it be true?" Asa commented. His lids drooped over his eyes, and almost instantly the old man was sound asleep, evidently worn out by the stirring events of the morning.

"Isn't it wonderful to think of the history Mr. Sidney has lived through?" Nancy mused. "He can remember when there were slaves. He has seen the kerosene lamp replace the candle, the gas light take the place of oil lamps. And now electric lights are found even in isolated farmhouses."

"Yes, and the stage coach develop into the airplane," Sadie replied. "He has seen the telephone, the radio, steam heat, electric ice boxes—oh, all the things we think we couldn't do without have come into use in his lifetime."

"At that, he hasn't seen human nature change very much," Nancy commented. "Sadie, didn't you ever tell him what you suspect about Mr. Semitt?"

"Oh, Nancy, how can I? I can't prove anything," the distressed girl whispered excitedly. "I don't want to be a tale-bearer. It would only make him unhappy."

"Yes, that is true," Nancy said. "Perhaps it will not be hard to find proofs for your suspicions, though. And have you considered that it is not only unfair to Mr. Sidney but to whomever he will make his heirs to let Mr. Semitt cheat him?"

"What shall I do?" Sadie cried. "I am so confused."

"Don't do anything," Nancy said impulsively, putting an arm over the frail girl's shoulders. "Let the whole sad business fade from your mind. I will talk it over with my father."

"He is such a splendid man," Sadie sighed. "You are so lucky to have a fine, famous person like Mr. Drew for your father, Nancy. I wish I knew who my parents were."

"Haven't I promised you that we shall settle that problem, too?" Nancy asked, patting the orphan as she rose. "Let's carry these things out quietly so Mr. Sidney can rest, and don't worry about a thing, Sadie. I have seen the most confused situations clear up just as soon as the key to the puzzle was found—and we'll find it this time!"

CHAPTER XIII

FROSTBITTEN FRIENDSHIP

NANCY found herself intruding upon an unhappy scene when she reached the porch. Frank Semitt was standing, pale and trembling, his fingers twisting nervously in his pockets, his back against the wall. Carson Drew was pacing the floor, his hands behind him, just as Nancy had often seen him in the court rooms.

"What was your income from the pasture lands last year?" Mr. Drew shot forth.

"Only about two hundred dollars," Semitt choked.

"Did you give Mr. Sidney an accounting of it?" Mr. Drew demanded.

"I spent the money fixing the place up."

"In general repairs to the building, or in the restaurant equipment?" Mr. Drew asked.

"I—I forget," Semitt said, wiping his brow. "General repairs, of course. Sure, that's right."

"The house hasn't been painted," Mr. Drew snapped. "The grounds are ill-kempt. The roof is weather-beaten. What improvements did you make?"

"Say, I ain't on no witness stand," Semitt snarled, sounding like a wolf at bay. "I ain't going to answer questions you ain't got no business askin' me."

"Very well, then," Mr. Drew replied with unexpected mildness. "Thank you for the coöperation you did extend to me."

Semitt's shifty eyes took on a gleam of cunning.

"I been working hard making a living for my family and keeping the old man clean and comfortable and well fed," he said. "If you think there's any crooked work going on, maybe you're right. I ain't saying nothing one way or another, but if I was you I'd keep an eye on them two guys who was here this morning, carrying on so disgraceful."

Nancy had not interrupted the interview, but kept still as a mouse in the doorway. Thus it was that Mrs. Semitt did not see her as she stole in from the kitchen and cautiously took up a position at a window close to where her husband was standing. Nancy, from her point of vantage, could see Semitt on the porch and the man's wife behind him in the house.

As Mr. Drew paced up and down, Mrs. Semitt raised the window little by little, each time his back was turned. Nancy saw the woman, using the cretonne curtain for concealment, crouch down at the opening and whisper something to her husband.

A relieved look came over the man's face;
then, keeping his eyes on Mr. Drew he cautiously pulled a bulky manila envelope from
beneath his jacket and held it behind him. Mrs.
Semitt's hand reached out for it.

"Yes, Mr. Drew," Semitt went on, "and
what's more, I think each one of them fellers
suspects the other of sneaking things out of the
old man's room. I don't know what they take,
because for all I know Mr. Sidney ain't got a
dollar in the world outside of this property."

Nancy stepped softly from her place of concealment and walked up behind Mrs. Semitt,
whose eager hand swooped out and snatched
the envelope from her husband's grasp. Frank
Semitt ostentatiously folded his arms and
moved away from the window, while his wife
surveyed the envelope he had passed to her,
and then turned noiselessly away.

On her face was a look of sneaking triumph
mingled with overwhelming curiosity, but that
expression was wiped away the second she
looked up and saw Nancy confronting her.

"What do you want, pussyfooting around?"
the woman snapped, her lips white.

"Nothing at all," Nancy said with an innocent air. "I was just looking for an envelope
—oh, you have found it, haven't you?"

"Not at all," Mrs. Semitt barked, concealing
the envelope beneath her apron. "This is for
me and it just came in the morning mail."

"Perhaps you made a mistake?" Nancy remarked. "May I look at the address?"

"You may not," Mrs. Semitt retorted. "I guess a body has a right to some privacy in her own house, even if it is open to the public."

She brushed past Nancy, only to confront Mr. Drew, who, attracted by the sharp tone of the voices, had entered the room to investigate.

"What is the trouble?" he asked.

"No trouble at all, thank you," Mrs. Semitt said. "Just a little misunderstanding."

"I happened to see Mr. Semitt pass an envelope in through the window when your back was turned," Nancy said.

Nancy's announcement was like a bombshell to Mrs. Semitt. In her agitation she dropped the envelope, and Nancy swiftly stooped and picked it up.

"There *is* a misunderstanding," she said. "This is addressed to Mr. Sidney after all. It isn't—" her voice grew sharp— "it isn't yours, is it, Mrs. Semitt?"

"N-no, I was just taking it up to the old gentleman," Mrs. Semitt said, blinking and running her tongue over her dry lips.

"Then I apologize for detaining you," Nancy smiled. "I see it is a registered letter from the Mid-Western Gas & Power Co., so it must be important."

Without another word Mrs. Semitt hurried up the stairs. Nancy, with a roguish wink at her father, asked him if it was not time to go home.

"Yes, my business here is finished," Carson Drew said, regarding his daughter with frank admiration. "You have just given me some very valuable information, whether you know it or not."

"I was trying to give you information on the chance that it might be valuable," Nancy replied. "I saw Semitt sneak that letter in to his wife, and if it hadn't been for that bit of luck I doubt if Mr. Sidney would ever have received it."

As Nancy drove the car home, Mr. Drew told her that among the assets Mr. Sidney had included in his estate were several shares of stock in the power company, but that the old man had expressed the belief they were worthless because he had received no dividends in four years.

"I have some of that stock myself," Mr. Drew said. "It is a sound and conservative investment, which always pays its dividends promptly, so I knew someone was intercepting Mr. Sidney's checks. If you had not performed that very clever piece of detective work it would have been hard to trace the theft or to prove it."

"Then do you suspect the Semitts of robbing Mr. Sidney?" Nancy asked.

"I am certain of it," Mr. Drew said with conviction. "Mr. Sidney did not know his home had been converted into a public inn until I told him. Gradually through the years the Semitts, whom he had employed as housekeepers and gardeners, have shunted him to the third floor, and his personal desire to be alone helped their scheme. Meanwhile, Semitt has rented out acres of the estate to local farmers and pocketed the money, I believe."

"Then let me add to your suspicions," Nancy said, slowing the car. "This morning I saw Semitt bury a wooden chest under a woodpile. When you sent me for Mr. Hill I unearthed the box first—it took only a minute—and I put it in a vault in the bank. I have a receipt for it."

"Nancy! That was rather high-handed," Mr. Drew said reprovingly. "It may contain Mr. Semitt's personal property."

"I don't think so, because it bore a label saying very plainly that the contents were valuable personal property of Asa Sidney," Nancy replied. "Furthermore, I recognized the box as one I saw in the old man's room last night."

"We will take Mr. Sidney to the bank to identify the box," Mr. Drew said. "If it was taken from his room, that alone is enough to put Semitt behind the bars. I am sorry that my confidence in you was a little shaken, Nancy dear. I ought to know by now that I can depend upon you."

Nancy smiled happily at her father's praise, and stepped on the accelerator to speed the car homeward.

Mr. Drew described some of his conversation with Mr. Sidney, and explained that the aged recluse was suspicious that his fortune was being tapped by thieving hands, although so cleverly he could not prevent it.

"He is rather contemptuous of money, although he is really a rich man," Mr. Drew said. "So long as he has his room and his meals and materials with which to experiment and mould candles, he does not care particularly about anything else—except one person."

"Sadie?" Nancy asked, as she drew the car to a halt in front of their beautiful home.

"There are some things I must keep secret even from you, Nancy," Mr. Drew said as he stepped from the car. "What a lawyer learns in confidence he must keep in confidence even from loving and trustworthy daughters. However, you will know everything eventually— everything, that is, except why Mr. Sidney wants to do a certain thing. That is a great mystery to me."

"More mystery?" Nancy cried, as she entered the house with her parent. "Oh, I wish you could give me just a hint, Dad—but no! I should not ask that. I know that your lips are sealed."

"It will tax your ingenuity when it is made

public," Mr. Drew said with a shake of his head.

"Speaking of added mysteries," Nancy said, "do you think we could find out who Sadie's parents were?"

Mr. Drew stared at his daughter oddly.

"You know she is an orphan," Nancy explained. "She was found in a church, she told me. The Semitts reared her, although I don't think they legally adopted her."

"One thing at a time, Nancy!" Mr. Drew chuckled. "We have an hour and a half before Hannah puts the dinner on the table, and I want to spend that time in going through some old files I have which may throw some light on angles of this case, I hope."

"Then I think I'll run downtown for a while," Nancy observed.

She changed into a lighter frock, for the afternoon had become warm and sultry. It was a simple and inexpensive dress of white silk which she had selected, with a loosely tied scarf of vivid blue sprinkled with a design of yellow blossoms for a touch of brightness. White stockings and white kid slippers completed the outfit, and Nancy made a very pretty picture indeed, with her fresh, natural color and crisp, golden hair as she reëntered her snappy little roadster and headed it toward the center of River Heights.

Nancy's objective was the home of her chum,

Bess Marvin. When she reached the modest dwelling place she noticed a familiar automobile parked in front. It was Peter Boonton's car.

For a moment Nancy debated whether to call for her friend or drive on to Bess's cousin, George Fayne, and discuss with her a visit to Asa Sidney. But then the matter was settled for her by seeing George cross the room that fronted on the street.

"Something seems to be on George's mind," Nancy thought as she pocketed the key to her car and started for the house. "I am sure she saw me, though she gave no sign of recognition."

Bess answered the doorbell. She smiled, almost as if in spite of herself.

"Hello, Nancy," she said, closing the door behind her and joining her friend in the open air. "Uncle Peter's inside. I hear you were at The Sign of the Twisted Candles again today."

"That's what I have come to talk to you about, Bess," Nancy exclaimed. "Call George, won't you? I have some exciting things to tell you, and we must plan another visit out there."

"Oh, I don't think I care to come," Bess replied airily. "And I'm sure George isn't interested."

Nancy flushed with disappointment and embarrassment at Bess's cool retort.

"Well, that's too bad," she said with a lump in her throat. "Dad has been retained as lawyer by Mr. Sidney, and some interesting problems have developed. We'd have fun tackling them."

"Oh, so your father is really taking sides in the case, is he?" Bess asked frigidly. "I'm sorry I must go help with the supper. Good-night."

Stung by the snub from her life-long friend, Nancy ran to her car and drove furiously toward home, tears brimming in her velvet-blue eyes. What had come over Bess? What sinister influence in the bitter Boonton-Sidney feud had brought this sorrow to her?

CHAPTER XIV

A Shocking Summons

"Good morning, Nancy. How do you feel this bright and lovely day?"

Carson Drew greeted his daughter at the breakfast table next morning with even more than usual good cheer, but there was an anxious light in his eyes as he scanned Nancy's face.

"Good morning. I'm feeling fine. Why shouldn't I?"

Nancy tried to make her smile appear its brightest as she seated herself at the table and poured her father's coffee. Her own pot of cocoa steamed at her plate, and the cool, bright sunshine that came through the broad windows seemed to be caught up and confined in the fragile glass of chilled orange juice before her.

"Did you sleep well?" Mr. Drew continued.

"Of course I did," Nancy replied. "Oh, good morning, Hannah. N-no, I don't think I'll have cereal this morning. And no egg, please. Just some toast."

"What's happened to your appetite?" Hannah asked.

"Nothing at all is the matter with me," Nancy smiled. "Perhaps it is the heat."

With a shake of her head and a murmured something about a dose of castor oil and a hot mustard foot-bath, Hannah left the room. Carson Drew, regarding his daughter quizzically over his plate, ate his breakfast thoughtfully. Nancy took practically nothing at all.

"Now then, partner!" Carson Drew said as he rose from the table and put an arm over Nancy's shoulders. "Out with it! Something is bothering you."

"Oh dear, you always find out everything," Nancy said with a sad little smile. "You can probably help me at that. Dad, for some reason connected with this Asa Sidney case George and Bess are angry with me—George won't speak to me at all and Bess snubbed me last night."

Nancy's lips quivered a little at the remembrance of the cruelly unexpected termination of the old friendship.

"That is too bad, too bad," Mr. Drew frowned, leading Nancy to the broad piazza and standing at the railing, staring thoughtfully into the massive old trees. "Some folks are hard to understand. Why should the Marvins and the Faynes poison the minds of their girls with a sordid old family feud so ancient it concerns none of them? It is pitiful. I don't know how to help you, Nancy. You will have to ac-

cept the situation as one of life's disappoint-
ments, and trust to Time to set matters right.''

"We never dreamed, the day we took refuge
at the tea room, that Asa Sidney was a relative of Bess and George,'' Nancy sighed.
"Peter Boonton, though, is probably striving
to get a part of Mr. Sidney's fortune, and
Jacob Sidney is trying to prevent him from getting any share.

"So I suppose both sides are suspicious of
you for being Mr. Sidney's counsel, and for that
silly reason George and Bess are forbidden to
be friends with me. Is that the way it appears
to you, Father?"

"That is the way matters are as I see them,''
Mr. Drew nodded. "You will have to let time
pass and events prove that neither you nor I
have meddled in the affairs of the family, I am
afraid.''

"I am disappointed in Bess and George,''
Nancy sighed again.

Mr. Drew looked at his daughter with com-
passion, and decided that the best way to mend
Nancy's hurt feelings was to lead the discussion
into other channels and get her interested in
problems other than her own.

"I really don't know how to go about this
case of Sidney's,'' he remarked. "It is a big
puzzle.''

Nancy became instantly alert.

"What is the trouble?" she asked.

"We must put a stop to the systematic pilfering that is draining his fortune," Mr. Drew said.

"Whom else do you suspect, besides the Semitts?" Nancy asked. "Peter Boonton and Jacob Sidney are surely not dishonest, no matter how greedy they are for their uncle's wealth."

"We can safely rule out Boonton and Sidney," Mr. Drew said. "You are right about that, Nancy. I think you found the answer to the problem in that box you dug up and put in the bank. If only we had a witness to Semitt's burying it. He will probably deny it, and testify that you had better chances than he had to spirit the chest out of Asa's room."

"Surely nobody would believe that I stole it just to get Semitt into trouble!" Nancy gasped.

"A clever and unscrupulous lawyer plus a stupid jury might put any interpretation on it," Mr. Drew replied. "I think the best thing to do is to have Mr. Sidney identify the box and check its contents at the bank first of all. Everything depends on that—far more than you, or even I with knowledge I cannot share with you, may now suspect."

Nancy's unhappy memories of Bess's cruel coldness vanished as her mind seized the new problem set forth by her father.

"Let us call on Asa Sidney this morning," she suggested. "Meanwhile there is another

clue to consider. Fingerprints! Semitt's must
be all over the chest!"

"Excellent! We—but there is the 'phone,"
Mr. Drew exclaimed. "I hope it is not some
summons to which I must give up my morning.
There is no time to be lost in the Sidney case.
It affects the future happiness of—well! Run
answer the telephone like a sweet girl!"

Nancy, knowing how often her father's plans
had been suddenly altered by a telephone mes-
sage, ran laughingly to the instrument, determined to inform anyone at all that Mr. Drew
was very busy.

Hannah had reached the telephone first, and
Nancy heard her say: "I can't hear you at
all! Who is this?"

"I'll take it, Hannah," Nancy said quietly,
and lifting the receiver to her ear she asked:
"Who is this? Miss Nancy Drew speaking."

"Oh, Nancy!"

The exclamation came faintly over the wire,
ending in a deep, shuddering sigh.

"Hello? Who is this? Who is speaking?
What is the matter?" Nancy cried.

"Nancy—something—something——"

"Is this Bess? Or George?" Nancy demanded.

"Nancy, this is—Sadie. Oh, please come at
once! Something awful has happened, I think.
O-oh!"

There was a sharp click, then silence.

Sadie had hung up, leaving Nancy in a state
of mingled surprise and alarm. She flew to
her father's side at once, and in a few words
described what she had heard over the telephone. Mr. Drew's face became very grave.

"We must go at once," he said instantly.
"I will be ready for you as soon as you bring
your car around in front."

A few moments later Nancy and her father
were speeding along the now familiar road to
The Twisted Candles, at a rate of speed very
close to the limit allowed by law. Few words
were exchanged between father and daughter,
for the mind of each was intent on the mysterious and urgent summons from Sadie.

What could have happened? Nancy thought
of a dozen answers. Perhaps Mrs. Semitt had
not kept her word and had told her husband of
Sadie's conversations with Nancy, resulting in
Sadie being driven from home. Perhaps Peter
and Jacob had met again, and had joined in a
pitched battle.

Nancy's mind raced faster than did the motor
of her car. At last the tower room of The
Twisted Candles could be seen above the trees,
and a minute later Nancy steered into the
sweeping driveway.

"Oh!" she gasped, applying the brakes.

Standing in the driveway was a long, black
automobile without windows. It was an under-
taker's ambulance. Someone was—dead.

Nancy did not wait for her father but ran to the house, entering without ceremony. She halted in her tracks at the sight of Sadie's huddled form on the bottom step of the big staircase, her head on her knees, her thin shoulders shaken with sobs.

"Sadie!" Nancy cried, sitting down beside the girl and clasping her in her arms. "What is the matter, dear?"

"Mis—Mister Su-su-Sidney," Sadie sobbed. "He died during the night. I found him—I thought he was asleep—when I brought his breakfast this morning."

"Mr. Sidney is dead," Nancy said soberly to her father, who had entered the hallway.

"Too bad, too bad," Mr. Drew said with a shake of his head. "It is true that he lived far, far longer than most persons, and his life was not a happy one. If only he had lived a few days more, though, what sorrow and trouble could have been averted!"

"Why Dad, what do you mean?" Nancy asked.

"I mean that the bickering relatives will now gather and begin to fight over the poor old man's earthly treasures," Mr. Drew said. "Not to mention others who are not related, but whose fingers have already fastened upon his property."

At this juncture Frank Semitt appeared with a long face.

"Mr. Sidney has gone to his just reward," the inn-keeper said in sepulchral tones. "He was gathered to his fathers during the night."

"I shall stay here as his executor and take charge," Mr. Drew said curtly.

"Who asked you to butt in?" Semitt snapped, dropping his assumed sorrow. "There's nothing to be done. We have the funeral arranged, and we'll even pay for it out of our own pockets!"

The man seemed bubbling over with aggressiveness and self-assurance. Asa Sidney's death seemed to have added immeasurably to Semitt's courage—and offensiveness.

Mr. Drew regarded him keenly, and determined to abide by his word and assume charge of the late Asa Sidney's personal effects. Soon the Sidneys and the Boontons would be gathering, fighting openly now for the fortune. Between them and justice stood only himself—and Nancy.

"And yet," Carson Drew mused, "if I had my pick of anybody in the state to stand by me, I don't think I would choose any other helpmate than Nancy!"

CHAPTER XV

Asa's Will

NANCY DREW has never forgotten that weird, wild day at The Twisted Candles, although she had had far more thrilling experiences before, and more exciting adventures since.

The frail body of the century-old inventor was gently carried out of the room which had been his whole world for years, and taken to the city for the brief interval before burial. Before that had been done the relatives began to arrive: Peter Boonton and his nieces, the mothers of Bess Marvin and George Fayne; Jacob Sidney and some stranger to whom he referred pointedly as his legal advisor.

Carson Drew, however, had taken his stand like a sentry at the door to Asa's room and allowed no one to enter. In the course of the morning a deputy from the sheriff's court arrived in response to Mr. Drew's summons and affixed a seal to the door of the Tower Room.

Poor Sadie was heart-broken. She had literally and actually lost her best friend in all the world, and sincere grief at the old man's departure was strengthened by the girl's anticipation of the empty, hard-working days and years before her.

Nancy did all she could to comfort Sadie, telling her that Mr. Drew had practically promised to find out the secret of her ancestry, and pledging herself to visit Sadie often and to have the girl spend weeks at her home. Nancy, you see, knew what it meant to lose friendship, and her heart still ached at the estrangement with Bess and George.

All interest, of course, centered upon Mr, Drew. The relatives pleaded and threatened, wept and scolded for a chance to enter Asa Sidney's room "just to pick up a small keepsake." Peter Boonton and Jacob Sidney waited their opportunities to speak to Mr. Drew privately, trying to learn what was in Mr. Sidney's will.

"I must comply with the law and with the ethics of my profession," was Mr. Drew's only response to all questions.

He did, however, have a longer conversation with the Semitts.

"You are held responsible for that room," he told them. "If that seal is broken you will be arrested. The windows are also locked and sealed so there is an additional responsibility to see that no one climbs in through them. Do you understand?"

Awestruck, the two Semitts pledged themselves to keep the chamber undisturbed.

At last Mr. Drew called all the relatives together and asked them to agree upon funeral plans. Nobody seemed very much concerned over the disposal of Asa Sidney's mortal remains, and it was swiftly decided to hold private ceremonies and inter the body in the River Heights cemetery, after Mr. Drew assured them that there were funds available in cash to pay the expenses.

"Then we will meet here in three days to open the will," Mr. Drew said. "First it must be filed for probate in the county court. Shall we agree to a meeting at this place three days hence, at two o'clock in the afternoon?"

"If that's the earliest, all right," Peter Boonton assented grumblingly.

Nancy at first entertained the idea of asking Sadie to her home for the three days, and then decided it would be far better if the girl remained to keep a watchful eye on the premises.

"You will do that, won't you, Sadie?" Nancy asked, and the girl nodded her tearful promise.

"I hope Mr. Sidney left the house to the Semitts, though," she said. "It is the only home I ever knew, and it is full of memories of his kindness to me. I should like to remain here—where I can see you often, Nancy."

"No one knows what is in the will but my father," Nancy replied. "But I am pretty sure that Mr. Sidney made some provision for you, Sadie. He seemed to love you too much not to remember you in some way or other."

When she drove her father home later in the day Nancy commented with distaste on the greed shown by the relatives.

"Most of them are pretty nice folks," she said sadly. "Mrs. Fayne and Mrs. Marvin have always been kind to me, and are as pleasant women as you would care to meet. They seemed entirely different persons today."

"It is certainly tragic what changes in a person's character can be made by competition for money, especially unearned money," Mr. Drew commented. "When this is all forgotten and the persons can become their natural selves again the petty meanness and jealousy will vanish again into the secret depths of their minds, perhaps forever. It is something we must all guard against in ourselves."

On each of the intervening days before the reading of the will Nancy found opportunity to drive to The Twisted Candles, first to see Sadie and secondly to examine the sealed door to convince herself it had not been tampered with. On the last day she encountered Peter Boonton on the grounds talking to a stranger.

"We could cut the place up into sixty building lots," Boonton was saying. "We will sell half to raise money enough to develop the rest, and build cottages and roads. Where the old house stands I plan to put up a modern gasoline station."

Then he saw Nancy, and abruptly shut his jaws with a click and led the real estate broker away.

"Counting his chickens before they are hatched," Nancy mused. "He seems very certain of getting the property!"

At last the day arrived when all interested persons met at The Twisted Candles for the reading of the will. They assembled in one of the ground floor dining rooms. George and Bess were there, nodding wistful greetings to Nancy but staying close to their parents.

Mr. Drew directed that the Semitts were to be present. Nancy went to hunt for Sadie, who was too grief-stricken to appear. Mrs. Semitt told her where the girl's room was, and Nancy, accustomed to her own tastefully furnished room with its tinted walls, its attractive drapes, its desk and easy chair and pleasant pictures, was shocked at the cell-like severity of Sadie's bedchamber.

It was a tiny room at one end of the second floor hall, with one window. The walls were painted an ugly shiny green. A straight-backed chair, an iron bed with some of the white enamel chipped off, and a varnished pine dresser completed the furnishings. Sadie had made fluffy curtains for the one window, and had pinned up gaily-colored magazine covers as an attempt at decoration.

Sadie herself was lying on the bed, her eyes

swollen from tears, when Nancy entered. She demurred at first against joining the expectant circle downstairs.

"You must come, Sadie," Nancy urged. "My father said you would have to be present. I am sure that means Mr. Sidney left you something in his will."

"I hope he gave me his old easy-chair, the one in which he loved to sit at the window," Sadie choked.

She dashed some cold water from the pitcher into her eyes, smoothed her plain dress and permitted Nancy to lead her downstairs. Sadie took a seat at the edge of the circle of whispering relatives, her eyes downcast in shyness. Nancy stood behind her, patting the girl comfortingly on the shoulder.

"We have met," Mr. Drew began to address the group, "to read the last will and testament of Asa Sidney. The document was written only a week ago, in his own hand and in duplicate. The original is filed in the court house and I hold the copy here. They have been carefully compared and found to be exact duplicates.

"The will was witnessed by Mr. Raymond Hill, executive vice-president of the Smith's Ferry Bank. I preface the reading of these papers with these remarks because some of its provisions may surprise you. I may add that, although I am named executor of the estate, I had never met nor even heard of Mr. Sidney twenty-four hours before I was summoned by him to help draw up this document.''

There was a stir in the group and a sudden hum of voices, which was quickly hushed as Mr. Drew opened a bulky envelope, and unfolded some crisp sheets of paper.

''Mr. Hill, will you identify this testament?''

The banker, who had been sitting unnoticed in one corner, arose, examined the papers, and nodded.

''That is my signature,'' he said. ''And those are my initials on each sheet. This is the document which Mr. Sidney prepared, and which I witnessed.''

''This identification is not legally necessary,'' Mr. Drew added. ''I requested it for a special purpose.''

''Hurry up with the reading and cut out the fancy business,'' Jacob Sidney called out.

Mr. Drew shot him a level look. Then he began to read, while everyone—Sadie excepted —leaned forward tensely.

'' 'I, Asa Sidney, being of sound mind, although in the hundred and first year of my life, do declare this to be my last will and testament, prepared by my own hand, legally witnessed.

'' 'The property which I wish disposed of after my death according to the terms stated hereinafter, is as follows:' ''

Nancy listened sharply as her father read off a long list of items, striving to memorize each one. True, she knew she could easily obtain a copy of the list from her parent, but the best place to keep the record was safely engraved upon her brain.

The house, with 400 acres of surrounding land, headed the list. Then came the full legal description of another piece of real estate in River Heights, a place Nancy instantly recognized as being in the heart of the business district and consequently very valuable.

Two bank accounts were mentioned, each containing over one thousand dollars, and also some shares in a building and loan company.

" 'The bank books and receipts are included in the contents of a black wooden chest bound in brass upon the lid of which is my name in my own hand,' " Mr. Drew read. " 'The chest is in my room. Also in my room——' "

Nancy gasped. The ebony box! The one Semitt had buried. She cast a quick look in the inn-keeper's direction and saw that he was looking stiffly out of the window—in the direction of the shed.

Lists of bonds and bank shares were tabulated in the will, and hoards of gold coin were referred to as being in one box or another, or in a drawer in some old desk or other piece of furniture.

" 'I do hereby direct,' " Mr. Drew read in a

voice suddenly a note or two louder, " 'that each of my descendants, namely Jacob Sidney, Peter Boonton, Anna Boonton Marvin and her daughter Bess Marvin, Louise Boonton Fayne and her daughter George Fayne, as well as the young woman known as Sadie Wipple, shall each select by mutual consent and in the order named one article of furniture from my belongings as a permanent keepsake.' "

"Oh, Nancy, he didn't forget me!" Sadie breathed. "Perhaps nobody will want that old easy chair and I may be allowed to keep it!"

" 'Excepting,' " continued Mr. Drew with emphasis, " 'that all my candle moulds and models for candles, lighting devices, lamps and so forth, and all the candles, shall first be destroyed under the supervision of Carson Drew, my legal advisor, who is hereby declared executor of the estate without bond.

" 'And excepting the portrait of my late and beloved, although estranged wife, which will be disposed of hereinafter.

" 'I then direct that all my other property, real and personal, be converted into cash by legal sale at the best possible price within thirty days after my death, and the money thus realized is to be divided into nine equal parts.' "

At this everyone sat up straight again, and calculating looks were exchanged among the possible heirs.

" 'One share shall again be divided into seven equal parts,' " Mr. Drew continued solemnly, and the now bewildered heirs sat further forward on their chairs. " 'One of these shares, that is, one sixty-third of the entire estate, shall be given to Frank Semitt and his wife, Emma, in consideration of those years during which they served me honestly and well.

" 'One each of the remaining sub-shares, namely one sixty-third of the entire estate, shall be given to each of my relatives, namely Jacob Sidney, Peter Boonton, Anna Marvin, Bess Marvin, Louise Fayne and George Fayne.

" 'All the rest of the money, to wit, eight-ninths of the cash proceeds of the estate, shall be given to the girl known as Sadie Wipple, who shall also inherit the portrait of my wife——' "

A concerted growl arose from the disappointed heirs.

"Quick, a glass of water!" Nancy cried. "Sadie has fainted."

CHAPTER XVI

PLOTS AND PLANS

"I WOULDN'T get that girl a drink if I owned all the water in the world and she was dying of thirst," Jacob Sidney snarled, folding his arms and glaring down at the unconscious Sadie.

"Here, you, get the girl a glass of water," Raymond Hill commanded Frank Semitt, who did not look as angered and disappointed as did the others. With a start of surprise Semitt jumped for the door and returned with a brimming tumbler of water, some of which Nancy sprinkled on Sadie's white face and some of which she forced between the girl's teeth.

Sadie stirred and sat up.

"I—I must have fainted," she murmured. "Oh, Nancy, there you are. Please don't go away."

Sidney and Boonton, Bess and George and their mothers were crowding toward the door muttering angrily among themselves.

"We'll fight this out in court," Peter Boonton shouted.

"You bet we will," Jacob Sidney seconded. "There isn't a court in the world that will uphold this fake will. Asa Sidney wasn't in his right senses when he cheated his own relatives and left his money to a nameless foundling!''

Mr. Drew made no reply to the threats, being busy conferring in an undertone with Raymond Hill. Sadie cringed at the harsh words hurled at her, and Nancy, her head erect, scowled her contempt at the furious men.

Bess and George, looking rather bewildered, left the house with their mothers, without even throwing a backward glance in Nancy's direction.

One by one the angry relatives departed. Mr. and Mrs. Semitt remained in the room.

"Oh, Sadie darling," Mrs. Semitt gushed. "It is all too wonderful for words. Poor dear, you look so white. Can't I bring you some iced tea?"

"I know what will make her feel good, and that is a cup of jellied chicken broth," Frank Semitt cried.

"I—I don't want anything, thank you," Sadie murmured. "I'm all mixed up in my mind. This was all so unexpected."

"Nonsense, we both hoped and planned that you would be rewarded this way," Mrs. Semitt smirked. "You deserved everything, Sadie, and all I can say is that I hope you won't forget your hardworking foster-parents who gave you a home, never anticipating any reward at all."

"Oh, I am grateful," Sadie replied.

"I think you had better not bother Sadie any more," Nancy told the Semitts. "She is all upset. Please go away and let her rest."

"Why, of course we will," Frank Semitt cried heartily. "We wouldn't want to intrude on her happiness at all, would we, Emma?"

"And besides, the house and all is Sadie's now," Mrs. Semitt added. "We must remember, Frank, that our little girl is quite wealthy, or will be soon."

"I'm sure you will have no trouble remembering that," Nancy commented dryly. "Come, Sadie, you will feel better if you sit on the porch where it is cooler."

Once outside and out of earshot of everybody, Sadie turned to Nancy and gripped her arms tightly.

"Oh, Nancy! Mr. Sidney left me a great deal, didn't he? Why did he do it? I am so worried now. All his relatives will think I wormed my way into his affections, and there will be a lawsuit and I will be made to answer all sorts of questions in front of hundreds of curious people!"

Nancy patted Sadie soothingly.

"Don't worry," she said. "Dad will look out for you. Mr. Sidney left you his property because he loved you, I am sure, and because the greedy squabbling of his relatives angered and fretted him."

Sadie sighed and bowed her head

"It was so loving and generous of him to make me his heir," she said, "but he did not know that he was making a great deal of trouble for me."

To Nancy's annoyance Frank Semitt reappeared, bearing tall glasses of iced tea for the girls and a dainty glass bouillon cup filled with quivering jellied chicken broth for Sadie. He served the girls, and then sat down affably on the porch railing.

"What are you planning to do, Sadie?" he asked. "You will probably have a great deal of money. I suppose you will stay here until the property is sold, won't you? Mother Semitt is making up a new bedroom for you in the big front room."

"Oh, I can't think," Sadie cried piteously. "It is all so new, so strange. I will do whatever Mr. Drew advises."

"Surely you don't have to consult strangers when you have two loving parents—even if they are not flesh-and-blood father and mother—to guide you," Semitt insinuated. "Not that I think that Mr. Drew would give you bad advice. No, indeed. There is probably none smarter than he in the state when it comes to law, is there, Miss Drew?"

"He is very clever in other respects, too," Nancy replied. "Especially in reading character."

At this juncture Mr. Drew and Mr. Hill

emerged from the house, still conferring earnestly. Mr. Drew called Nancy to him, and suggested that she remain with Sadie for the time being.

"Not only does she need a companion, but some responsible person must keep an eye on the house and its contents, and there is no one I would trust more to prevent any crooked work from succeeding than you, Nancy," the lawyer said.

"Shall I drive you home first?" Nancy asked. "I really ought to get another dress and a nightgown if I am to stay here over night."

"Mr. Hill will drive me back," Carson Drew said. "I think you had better borrow a sleeping garment from Sadie, and get along as best you can, Nancy. I wouldn't leave this house alone to the Semitts for ten minutes."

Nancy was thrilled at the assignment. She followed her father to the automobile and then bade him goodbye. Upon returning to the house she saw that Sadie had left the porch, and set out to look for her.

The Semitts, too, seemed to have vanished, and Nancy walked cautiously, thinking that she might come upon the inn-keeper or his wife unawares and catch them in some scheming. A tour of the ground floor revealed no one there, so Nancy stole up the steps.

"Frank Semitt said that his wife was preparing another room for Sadie—the big front room, I think he said," Nancy mused. "We'll have a look in there."

A murmur of voices from behind a partly closed door caused her to move cautiously as she approached. It was Mrs. Semitt, speaking earnestly.

"—those quaint old chests, you know," Mrs. Semitt was saying. "If they are put up for sale they will not bring a dollar apiece, and yet I am quite crazy about them."

"The room is sealed, Mother Semitt," Sadie was heard to reply. "I couldn't give them to you if I wanted to, and I am sure I should have to ask Mr. Drew's permission first."

"Oh, shucks, Sadie! Don't be such a scared-cat!" Mrs. Semitt spoke. "Frank and I will just move out a few of the things we like awfully well, and no one will be the wiser. Besides, you shall have them as much as we, don't you see? We'll have them in our new home."

"What new home?" Sadie asked.

"You heard them say this place had to be sold," Mrs. Semitt answered. "So of course we will have to move. And with all your money you will want to select a nice, charming residence for us. You can trust Father Semitt to pick a bargain."

"Aha!" said Nancy to herself. "The Semitts are spending Sadie's inheritance for her already! If they have their way Sadie will be penniless and dependent on them in a few months."

Boldly she opened the door.

"Hello, Sadie, I thought you would be up here," Nancy said cheerfully. "What a charming room! I wonder if I might spend the night with you?"

"Oh, Nancy, would you do that, really?" Sadie exclaimed, clapping her hands. "How lovely!"

Mrs. Semitt regarded Nancy sourly, and with a sniff turned and left the room. Nancy listened carefully until she assured herself that the woman was going downstairs.

"Dad said I might stay if you invited me, and I want to stay so much I just invited myself," Nancy laughed.

The two girls examined the room together, in which Mrs. Semitt had assembled some of the choicest articles of furniture in the house as well as the best linens and draperies. Yet to the forefront of Nancy's mind was ever the responsibility placed upon her by her father of guarding the property.

When the two girls descended the stairs arm in arm half an hour later Nancy's sharp eyes missed two heavy brass candle-sconces ornamented with cut crystal pendants, which had been in the lower hall and which scores of collectors who had visited The Twisted Candles had attempted to buy.

"Sadie, I think things are beginning to disappear already," Nancy remarked. "Do please keep a sharp watch and tell me if you find anything familiar missing. There must be hundreds and hundreds of dollars' worth of antiques here, small pieces which could be quickly removed."

Sadie's untrained eyes, however, were not as keen as Nancy's, though much more familiar with the house. Nancy had to point out the missing sconces before Sadie realized they were gone.

"I think I'll prowl around a bit," Nancy announced.

All the shades in the house had been drawn, and a crudely-lettered sign on the door proclaimed that The Twisted Candle Inn was closed. The gloom, intensified by the shade of the thick-growing trees, made the great, empty building a weird and ghost-like place.

Nancy retraced her footsteps to the second floor and then continued directly to the Tower Room. As she had half feared, half expected, Frank Semitt was crouched at the door of the late Asa Sidney's room, studying the intricate lead seal placed there by the sheriff. The light of a twisted candle, carefully shaded so it would fall only in one direction, cast flickering shadows on the white walls.

"Oh, there you are, Mr. Semitt," Nancy said pleasantly.

The startled man wheeled on his heels, knocking the candle over.

"Did you lose another dime up here?" Nancy continued. "If it rolled under the doorway I'm sure it would be wisest if you waited until the door was opened by court order, instead of picking the seal."

"You must be crazy," Semitt snapped. "I was just making sure none of them sneaking relatives crept up here to burglarize the place, that's all."

"And did you find everything secure?"

"Oh, yes," growled Semitt, picking up his candle and rushing downstairs past the girl.

Nancy followed the man to the ground floor and saw him enter the kitchen, from which there presently arose the tones of the Semitts in earnest conference. Their words could not be overheard, however. Then the back door opened and closed, and Nancy concluded that the couple had left the house.

She returned to Sadie, and suggested that they stroll around the grounds. The weedy lawn and littered back yard were not attractive, and the ramshackle old shed which served Semitt as a garage and store-house did not lend any value to the scene so far as beauty goes.

The flicker of candlelight inside the place, however, made Nancy give the tumble-down structure close attention. Casually she led

Sadie into the woods on the spoken pretext of looking for flowers.

"We can't be seen from here," Nancy told her new friend. "We'll watch that shed and see what comes out of it."

"What could come out of it except Frank Semitt or his car?" Sadie asked wonderingly.

As if in response to her query the inn-keeper stepped out of the building and craftily surveyed the house and yard. Then he ducked back inside and presently emerged with two long boxes which he carried with difficulty, one under each arm.

"See where he goes," Nancy whispered. "He is going away from the road. What lies back there?"

"Just pastures and meadows and the old tenant farmer's house," Sadie whispered back.

"We will follow him," Nancy decided. "Can we get to the old house without leaving the woods?"

"It is a roundabout way," Sadie said, "but I can lead you."

Treading carefully so as to make no sound the two girls traversed the thicket. Soon Semitt was out of sight, but still Nancy urged Sadie on, convinced that the deserted old tenant house was Semitt's goal. After fifteen minutes of heavy going Sadie stopped and pointed.

"There's the old place," she said. "And

Nancy, you uncanny mind-reader, there is
Semitt just coming out of it!"

"We will wait until he is out of sight and
then search the cottage," Nancy decided.

It was a musty, dusty old building which
they entered. The light from the setting sun
struggled dimly through cobwebby and dusty
windows. The floor was thick with dirt and
fallen plaster.

"Ah, the footprints go directly upstairs,"
Nancy whispered, crouching to examine the
floor.

Up the creaking, wobbling old stairs the two
girls crept, their hearts thumping with excitement.

The second floor of the structure was just
unplastered attic. An old trundle-bed with a
corn-husk mattress moldered under the eaves,
and an ancient linen press, its doors awry and
its once fine mahogany surface green with
mildew, leaned against the chimney.

Nancy looked first into the huge wardrobe.

"It's as big as a house!" she cried. "All
the shelves have been taken away. I have seen
kitchens in apartment houses no bigger than
this."

The closet was obviously empty, though, so
she turned to examine the floor minutely. No
dust had settled here, because wind and rain
had easy access through the broken shingles.

"Oh, it's getting so dark," Sadie whispered.

"We'll go in a minute," Nancy said. "As soon as—aha! Here we have it!"

She knelt, and with her slim finger-tips drew the nails from one of the wide floor-planks.

"There was more litter on this board than on any other, but the cracks around it were clean," Nancy explained. "That proved to me the dirt was scattered deliberately, to make it look undisturbed—and besides, the nails are loose."

She pulled up the plank. Sadie gasped!

Four boxes were revealed to them, two of them obviously the ones Semitt had just brought. Nancy stooped to throw back the lid of the nearest one when a step suddenly creaked upon the stairs!

CHAPTER XVII

The Quarrel in the Farmhouse

"Oh, it is Father Semitt! He will kill us for spying on him," Sadie chattered, clutching at Nancy.

"He will have a hard job of it," Nancy said grimly under her breath. "This way, quick!"

She popped Sadie into the moldering old linen press, crowded in beside her, and pulled the doors as nearly shut as possible.

The stairs creaked again under the weight of someone slowly mounting them. Sadie gripped Nancy's arm, trembling violently, as a figure appeared at the head of the steps and paused to survey the attic.

"That isn't Semitt," Nancy whispered.

"Oh, I'm afraid to look," Sadie sighed. "I have my eyes shut tight, and there is a spider on my neck."

"Sh-sh-sh!" Nancy warned. "Don't move."

The man entered the attic and gave a start as he saw the displaced floor board. He crouched down to look into the opening, and evidently lifted the lids of the boxes. Then he straightened up and scanned the entire chamber. As his face was revealed in the dim light Nancy almost gave vent to a startled exclamation.

The man was Raymond Hill, the wealthy banker from Smith's Ferry, her father's associate in making Asa's will.

What was he doing here? Had he betrayed Carson Drew's trust and confidence? Had the lure of old Asa's fortune overcome his scruples, too? Nancy was tense as these questions raced through her mind.

Meanwhile, Mr. Hill paced slowly around the attic. Nancy was certain he would eventually pull open the doors of the antique and reveal Sadie and herself.

A plank creaked under Mr. Hill's feet and he stopped, stooped, and gave a little chuckle. Nancy saw him pry the nails loose and lift the board. He reached down into the opening and pulled out a metal document box, which sprang open on a touch. From it Mr. Hill took a bundle of papers which Nancy recognized at once as being bonds. He looked through them, stuffed the bundle into his pocket, and replaced the loose flooring, after kicking the box out of sight.

Nancy was in agony. Her feet were asleep from standing so still in such a cramped place. She was sure a dozen spiders had made a toboggan slide of her back-bone.

Mr. Hill's eyes roved about the attic and at

last lighted on the old linen press. He began to walk toward it slowly, testing the planks beneath his feet at every step.

Nancy was undecided whether to bravely emerge from the hiding place or gamble with the chance that Mr. Hill would not open it, when a more sinister sight chilled her blood.

Standing at the head of the steps, up which he had crept with practiced caution, was Frank Semitt! His eyes gleamed like a cornered rat's, and Nancy saw that he was undecided whether to accost Mr. Hill or to retreat.

At that moment Mr. Hill let his eyes sweep the attic once more, and Nancy saw him stiffen as he detected Semitt.

"Ah there, Mr. Semitt," Mr. Hill said sarcastically. "What are you bringing up here now? Come, let me see what is in that box!"

Semitt mounted the last step and strode toward Mr. Hill. In his arms he carried a square box tightly wrapped in old newspapers.

"I don't know what you are doing up here, trespassing around," Semitt snarled. "But if you want to see what I have, here it is!"

To Nancy's horror he hurled his burden full at Mr. Hill. The banker ducked and a corner of the heavy box caught his shoulder, causing him to lose his balance and almost fall.

That was the advantage Semitt wanted. Although Mr. Hill was twenty years older than the inn-keeper, and a smaller man, Semitt rushed forward with flailing fists. Mr. Hill threw up his arms to protect his face, whereupon Semitt thrust out a foot and tripped the banker, who fell heavily to the floor. In a flash Semitt was on top of him, one hand gripping Mr. Hill's throat and the other pounding his face and head.

"Oh, the coward!" Nancy exclaimed, and burst out of the wardrobe. She stumbled and almost fell as a feeling like pins and needles shot through her ankles. Conquering her discomfort the girl flew at Semitt and seized his shirt-collar at the back with both hands.

"Hi! Who's that? What?" Semitt choked. He craned his neck, and when he saw that Nancy was his new opponent he bared his teeth and snarled:

"Let go of me, you little sneak-thief, or I'll do worse than this to you."

Nancy's response was to twist her fingers deeper into the man's collar and tug the harder. Realizing that he had an unexpected ally, Mr. Hill squirmed free from Semitt's grasp and drove his fist deep into the inn-keeper's stomach.

Semitt straightened out with a gasp, his breath knocked out of him. Mr. Hill then arose, his clothing dirty and rumpled, his face rapidly swelling with discolored bruises.

"Why, Nancy! And Sadie, too! How did you get here?" the banker gasped.

"We were here first," Nancy said. "We heard you coming, and not knowing who it was we hid in the antique over there."

"To think of that!" Mr. Hill groaned. "Then did you pull up that loose plank over there?"

"Yes, we were just going to look in the boxes when you frightened us," Nancy replied.

Mr. Hill shook his head, and what was meant for a smile appeared on his battered features.

"Nancy, I owe you not only thanks but an apology," he said. "I was afraid your father was giving you a bigger job than you could handle when he put you on watch here, so I came back determined to spend the night prowling about to be on hand in an emergency.

"I saw Semitt coming from this direction and retraced his path to find out what he had been up to, away back here. I found the old house—and you know the rest!"

Semitt, clutching his middle, rose shakily to his feet.

"Shall I call the police, Sadie, and have this man arrested?" he asked painfully.

"Arrest me?" shouted Mr. Hill.

"Arrest Mr. Hill? Why?" Sadie and Nancy gasped in chorus.

"Why, for trying to steal old man Sidney's valuables, of course," Semitt replied. "Why else do you think he was poking around here, where Mr. Sidney used to hide his things?"

"Of all the false statements!" the banker bellowed, losing his dignity. "You are the thief! I know all about you."

"Ha ha! Deny if you can that you took a sheaf of bonds from under the floor and have them in your pocket this minute!" Semitt challenged.

"I don't deny it at all, and here are the bonds," Mr. Hill declared, disclosing the securities. "I didn't steal them. Whoever hid them there stole them."

"Tell that to the judge," jeered Semitt. "Old Asa hid them there himself!"

"May I see the bonds?" Nancy asked.

She examined the papers carefully—twelve crisp engraved bonds of five-hundred-dollar denomination each, and each one issued by the Mid-Western Gas & Power Co.

"These are the bonds that arrived in the mail the day before Mr. Sidney died," she said, returning them to Mr. Hill. "So he did not put them here himself at all. Those issues were in the envelope which you, Mr. Semitt, passed through the window to your wife!"

Semitt looked exactly as if he had received another blow on the chin.

"P-p-prove it!" he spluttered.

"Deny it if you can!" Nancy cried, stamping her foot.

Semitt shook his head in mock dismay.

"Come along, Sadie," he said. "Both these

would-be smart crooks are trying to rob you of your inheritance. Come on back to the house, and I will drive to River Heights at once and ask for a county detective to guard you, and we'll hunt up a lawyer without smarty daughters.''

''No, I don't ever want to be with you again,'' Sadie cried, throwing her arms around Nancy. ''Go away, please, and stay away!''

''You'll be sorry you said that some day, my fine lady,'' Semitt said with a forced laugh. ''When these new friends of yours have stripped you of everything you own except your oldest clothes, then you'll come around begging Frank and Emma to be good to you again.''

Nancy looked at Semitt from under level brows.

''There is a little matter of an ebony box with brass binding that was put under a woodpile,'' she said slowly. ''The story that chest can tell might mean that any visits you will have from Sadie will be in the state penitentiary!''

Semitt opened his mouth one or twice, then turned and marched down the dark stairs.

CHAPTER XVIII

NANCY TAKES CHARGE

"QUICK, we must follow closely behind him," Nancy cried, stooping to pick up the bundle Semitt had hurled at Mr. Hill.

"What are you going to do, call the police?"

"No, but I shall call up my father and report to him," Nancy said. "I don't want Semitt to cut any telephone wires or to injure my car."

Mr. Hill took the bundle from Nancy, and the three trailed Semitt across the meadow to The Twisted Candles.

"Now, if you will keep Mr. and Mrs. Semitt in sight, Mr. Hill," Nancy said, "I will telephone to Dad and tell him what has happened."

"Aye, aye, Mademoiselle," Mr. Hill laughed, executing a snappy salute. He followed Frank Semitt into the kitchen, and Nancy soon heard the excited tones of the inn-keeper and his wife raised in argument with the banker.

She ran to the telephone and called her home. Hannah answered, and to Nancy's consternation reported that Mr. Drew had left for a neighboring state in connection with the Sidney will case, and would not be back until the next afternoon.

"I'll have to stick it out, then," Nancy told herself grimly.

She returned to Sadie's room and asked that young woman to please summon Mr. Hill. When that rather dishevelled person appeared Nancy explained that her father was beyond reach for the time being.

"I don't doubt that Semitt has taken other valuables and secreted them around the place," she said. "I am also afraid that he is now enraged against Sadie and it is dangerous for her to stay here. Will you take her to your home, or to mine, Mr. Hill? I will stay here on guard."

Raymond Hill whistled.

"Oh, I shouldn't think of such a thing," he declared. "I am sure that man Semitt and his wife are capable of going to any extremes for money. I think you and Sadie ought to go home together."

"I can't do that," Nancy said. "I promised my father I would stay here and watch the place. If none of us remains the Semitts might strip the house of all its valuables and clear out."

"Better that than to suffer physical injury," Mr. Hill advised.

"No, I shall stay here," Nancy said firmly.

"I shall remain with you," Sadie declared.

"That leaves me no choice," the banker smiled. "I, too, shall remain all night."

Nancy reflected soberly for a moment.

"Mr. Hill, would you be willing to take the robes from my machine and camp out in the deserted farmhouse for the night to prevent Semitt from taking away any of the valuables he has hidden there?"

"Willing? I jump at the opportunity," Mr. Hill cried. "I always did say I was cut out to be a detective or a member of the Northwest Mounted Police. Banking is not an exciting profession," he sighed.

"Sadie and I will stay here and keep as wide awake as we can," Nancy continued. "We'll see that Asa Sidney's room is not unsealed and rifled."

It was quite dark now, and Nancy coolly summoned Mrs. Semitt and ordered food.

"Mr. Hill is leaving immediately after he has some supper," she said. "So please let us have something to eat—a cold supper will do—as soon as you can."

"Very well, Miss," said the woman stiffly, and left the room. The two girls and Mr. Hill chatted about the excitement of the afternoon in a general way, not caring to be caught in any plans by the eavesdropping Semitts.

Minute after minute passed. A quarter of an hour, then a full half hour.

"It is taking them a dreadfully long time to prepare supper," Nancy remarked.

"I'll run down and see how they are getting along," Sadie said.

"It is dangerous for you to go alone," Nancy declared. "I will go with you."

The kitchen, however, proved to be empty, and there were no signs of supper in progress to be seen. The meaning came to Nancy in a flash.

"The Semitts have run off," she exclaimed. "Get Mr. Hill quickly. Bring him out to my car at once."

Nancy flew out of doors to where her roadster was parked. Her worst fears were realized when she saw that both rear tires had been slashed with a sharp knife.

"And I have only one spare tire," she thought, vexed with herself for permitting the Semitts to outwit her at this point in the game.

Sadie and the banker appeared, and even as Nancy was telling them of the misfortune an idea came to her.

"That tire-cutting was done to prevent pursuit," she said. "Or else it was done to make us believe pursuit is necessary. I'll wager that the Semitts are not far off!"

Sadie ran to the corner of the house and immediately came back to report that the Semitt car was gone.

"They took nothing from the house, unless it

was secreted somewhere in the kitchen or basement," Nancy said. "What was in the boxes at the old farm house, Mr. Hill, besides the bonds?"

"A large chest of silverware, sterling, and a box of most beautiful table-linens," Mr. Hill replied. "I am sure the building is filled with loot."

"Then that's where the Semitts would go first," Nancy said with conviction. She jumped into her car and took a portable spot-light from the tool compartment.

"Now let's hurry to the farmhouse," Nancy said. "We'll leave the lights on my car burning, and a few in the house, to make it look as if the place was not deserted."

Nancy's remarkable sense of direction served her well as she strode off through the uplands and meadows to the old cottage. She was somewhat disappointed to find it in utter darkness.

"They got here ahead of us," Mr. Hill said. "If they came here at all."

"Wait a minute," Nancy said. "If they parked their car somewhere along the road it must have taken them as long, if not longer, to reach here as it took us."

The three stood in utter silence close to the trunk of a towering sycamore tree, a spot chosen by Nancy because she said the girls' airy dresses would merge with the light, mottled background of the trees in the darkness.

At last there came to Nancy's sharp ears a tiny sound that was at variance with the noises of myriads of insects and breezes and small animals. It was a metallic sound, muffled and distant.

Instantly she switched on her powerful flashlight, and the three hundred foot beam cut through the blackness like a silver sword. The tumble-down farmhouse sprang into view, and on the rickety front steps Frank and Emma Semitt were etched sharply in the glare.

"Call to them that the house is guarded and that they must leave at once," Nancy whispered to Mr. Hill. "Try to make your voice extra deep."

Raymond Hill chuckled, cleared his throat, and then in a resounding voice shouted the warning Nancy had dictated.

"Who are you, anyhow?" Semitt yelled back. "I got a right to be here!"

"Stand where you are," he continued, but Semitt only gave an ugly laugh in response and moved a step higher.

"If we could frighten them," whispered Nancy, "with a loud noise, such as——"

"Um—yes."

Nancy picked up a smooth stone. "I wonder——"

Mr. Hill quickly sensed her idea, grabbed the rock and with a straight fling he sent it forward at a swift pace.

There was the crash of splintered glass, and Semitt leaped off the steps into the darkness as the fan-light over the front door shattered into splinters, just as Nancy had hoped. Mrs. Semitt screamed and ran after her husband. Inexorably, Nancy kept the spot-light upon the panic-stricken pair as they charged through the brush and meadow grass toward the road.

"I guess they won't be back," Mr. Hill said with a laugh. "But just to be on the safe side I'll camp out here."

Nancy left the flashlight with the adventurous banker and returned to the house with Sadie, who was on the verge of hysterics as a result of the fateful day. From a drudging life in a roadside inn she had come into one of wealth and envy and had participated in a man-hunt, all in a few hours.

Nancy switched the lights off her car, and then entered the house. She directed Sadie to bolt all the windows, and as extra precaution she piled furniture against the doors.

"No burglar alarms, I suppose?" Nancy observed. "We'll have to invent some."

From the sideboard she took long-stemmed goblets and balanced them on the tops of the lower window sashes, so that any attempt to force the windows would send the glasses toppling to the floor with a crash.

"Go on to bed, Sadie. I'll sleep here on the couch," Nancy directed. Sadie demurred at being left alone, however, and at last the girls dozed off into uneasy slumber on pillow-piled settees.

Nothing happened to disturb their slumbers, and Nancy awoke, a little stiff and sadly rumpled, as the sun poured in through the windows. She found her way to the kitchen, washed her face and rinsed her parched mouth. Through the window she saw Mr. Hill making his way toward the house.

"Cheerio!" the banker hailed her. "All quiet on the battle front last night. Any excitement?"

"Not a bit," Nancy replied.

Sadie appeared and ventured the opinion she could make up a breakfast of sorts. While Mr. Hill telephoned to his home and his office Sadie made coffee which had to be drunk black by the banker, while milkless cocoa served for the girls. Scrambled eggs and toasted stale bread completed a filling, if not satisfactory meal.

"I shall have to go to the bank," Mr. Hill said. "My chauffeur will call for me, and then I am sending him back to mount guard at the farmhouse."

"We will stay here in the inn, which we will not open to anyone," Nancy planned. "As soon as my father returns I will have him see that a watchman is placed here, and I will take Sadie to my home."

"An excellent plan, certainly the best possible under the circumstances," Mr. Hill declared. "Nancy, you are a regular general. You certainly won a major battle of wits from the Semitts."

Nancy thanked Mr. Hill with modesty, and then the banker's car arrived and carried him off. The two girls were left alone to hold the fort. In half an hour's time the chauffeur was back again with new tires for Nancy's car, which he deftly mounted and pumped up before taking up his guard duty at the farmhouse.

Toward noon Nancy called her home and learned that her father had just arrived half a minute before. She swiftly outlined the events of the preceding day to him, and he promised that precautions such as Nancy suggested would be promptly taken. And indeed, within the hour, an automobile drove up with Mr. Drew in it, besides two powerfully-built men who walked as stealthily as cats.

"Private detectives," Mr. Drew said briefly.

He posted the men, one in the house and one at the farmhouse, to relieve the banker's chauffeur. At midnight they were to be relieved by another sentry.

"Now then, Sadie, pack your things and we'll speed home to a bracing bath and some real food," Nancy laughed happily. "Our worries are over for the time being!"

There Nancy made a mistake.

Not until she was at home did Mr. Drew tell

her that the Sidney-Boonton families had engaged Walker Cochran, a lawyer whose reputation was almost as great as his own, to fight
Sadie's claim to Asa Sidney's fortune.

"That's a contest where I can't help you,
can I?" Nancy asked. "I wish I were old
enough to be a lawyer!"

"You have done the work of a dozen men already," Mr. Drew said earnestly. "And I am
sure we shall win the lawsuit. It would help
very much if we had some supportable testimony as to why Mr. Sidney favored this orphan
girl above his entire family."

"It is not really his family, Dad," Nancy
said. "Mr. Sidney's children left no descendants. The Boontons and the Sidneys are just
branches of the family."

"Even so, they would be the heirs at law if
he had not made a will," Mr. Drew replied.

Nancy secretly resolved that she would search
for supporting evidence to the will to convince
the jury that Sadie had genuinely earned the
old man's gratitude.

"The Semitts, I learn, have joined with the
others to break the will," Mr. Drew went on.
"They may give dangerous testimony, if they
think it is worth their while, against Sadie."

"They are just trying to cover their guilty
tracks," Nancy said hotly. "You will certainly be able to batter down their stories."

"I hope so," Mr. Drew said.

Thoughtfully, Nancy returned to the guest room to help Sadie unpack.

That pathetically small job had already been accomplished by the new heiress. She had only three dresses, two of them serviceable black frocks to be worn while waiting on tables, and one a cheap flowered organdie, the same one she had worn to the house. Her small stock of undies and stockings did not half fill one bureau drawer, and the only shoes she had were the ones on her feet.

"Let's go downtown and have a shopping orgy," Nancy cried. "I have charge accounts, and you can pay me back when you receive your inheritance, Sadie. We'll buy some frocks and socks and slippers and silk underthings and pajamas."

"Oh, may I do all that?" Sadie gasped. "It will be the biggest thrill of my life."

"It'll be such fun for me," Nancy laughed. "Let's go at once."

Fun? As Nancy led Sadie into the elevator of a big department store, she discovered that Bess and George were the only other occupants!

CHAPTER XIX

AN ENCOUNTER AND AN INSPIRATION

THE two cousins smiled timidly at Nancy; then, as if remembering instructions, they drew themselves stiffly erect, their noses in the air. Sorrow tugged at Nancy's heart as she found herself snubbed once more for reasons that really mattered not at all either to herself or to her former chums.

Impulsively Nancy put her hand on Bess's arm gently.

"Bess," she said softly, "I have done nothing to you. Why must our friendship be broken because of a foolish quarrel that persons now dead had fifty years ago?"

To Nancy's surprise a big tear rolled down Bess's cheek. The girl shook Nancy's hand from her arm and turned her back, but her head was bowed and a sob shook her shoulders. George, meanwhile, bit her lip nervously, glancing from Bess to Nancy.

"We can't help it, Nancy," she said finally. "Your father is doing his best to keep our family from its just share in the estate."

The floor where women's clothing was displayed was reached, and Nancy suggested to Bess and George that they all sit down together in the lounge provided by the store for the comfort of weary shoppers.

"Let's talk this over a little," she said. "You should get acquainted with Sadie, too. Even if you decide not to remain friends with me, it won't harm you to know Sadie better."

Hesitatingly the cousins agreed, and soon the four girls, all but Nancy feeling acutely uncomfortable, were gathered in a corner of the rest room.

"Bess, you and George met Sadie the same evening I did," Nancy said. "We were all together then. It was the first time any of us met Mr. Sidney. Although he was a distant relative of you both, you had never heard of him. Isn't that so?"

Bess and George nodded, and Nancy continued:

"Sadie knew my father was a lawyer because I told her so. You were both with me when I told her, I think. It doesn't matter, because the only reason why I happened to mention it was to tell her there might be a way to trace her parentage. The very next morning after our visit to The Twisted Candles Sadie telephoned to me and said that Mr. Sidney had asked her to find a lawyer, and the only one she knew about was my father.

"Mr. Sidney wanted to make his will, and

seemed perfectly competent to do so. He didn't
seem to you to be unbalanced, did he?"

Bess and George looked at each other uncom-
fortably, then shook their heads in unison.

"It is my father's duty to carry out his
client's wishes," Nancy went on. "He is legally
bound to do so. He could be disbarred and
thrown out of his profession if he did not do it.
He would have to apply to the courts for permission to abandon the trust and give good
reasons for quitting.

"That is my side of the story. Sadie's is
just as simple. Ever since she was just a little
girl she has waited on Mr. Sidney, up until the
day he died. He chose to make her his heiress.
It hasn't brought her happiness. I know Sadie
would rather know who she is and who her
parents were, than to have every cent of Asa
Sidney's money without dispute."

"Oh, that is really true," Sadie cried sin-
cerely.

"I know the story of the family feud," Nancy
continued. "Now everyone who participated
in the original quarrel is dead. Why should we
let the foolish anger of persons who are no
longer living come between us?"

"Nancy," George said with decision, "you
are right. I might add that you are right as
usual. I, for one, am sorry and ashamed.
Please accept my apology, and take me back
as your friend. And what is more, I shall tell

Great-Uncle Peter at once that I have apologized to you!"

Bess, the plumper and more sensitive of the cousins, was frankly weeping into her handkerchief.

"Oh, Na-na-Nancy," she said, laughing through her tears, "I'm s-s-so glad we are friends again."

Nancy laughed aloud in sheer joy, and the others joined in. Women looked at the quartette with smiles, perhaps wondering what innocent little joke was amusing the young people.

"What are you shopping for?" George asked. "We always have so much fun buying things together."

"Sadie wants to get some new clothes," Nancy explained. "Want to help?"

"May we, Sadie?" Bess asked.

"I'd be very glad if you would," Sadie replied, smiling happily. "I really don't know much about styles."

When the store closed that evening, four gay young women left its portals, chatting merrily and laden with bundles.

Sadie had been re-outfitted from top to toe in attractive clothes which wrought a transformation in the thin, wan-looking girl. She seemed to have gained self-confidence with her new attire, too, but she was not yet entirely at ease.

"Please don't go far from me," she whispered to Nancy. "I'm afraid the Semitts may grab me, or do me some sort of harm."

"Don't worry," Nancy said airily, although privately she admitted to herself that Sadie's fears were well grounded. Frank Semitt would not be above kidnaping Sadie, she believed, or, more cannily, swearing that he was her legal guardian and getting a court order to put her in his power.

"We shall have to find out who Sadie really is," she decided. "That will be a big help."

After dinner at the Drew household Nancy helped Sadie unpack her new wardrobe, and they admired all over again each item of dress.

"I don't want to bring up anything unpleasant, but do you remember the name of the orphanage from which the Semitts took you?" Nancy asked.

"I was certainly reminded of it often enough," Sadie replied with a trace of bitterness in her voice. "I don't know how often one or the other would tell me how grateful I ought to be and how much harder I ought to work because The Twisted Candles was paradise compared with the New Fernwild Orphan Asylum."

"The New Fernwild Orphan Asylum," Nancy repeated. "Do you remember where it was located?"

"N-no, except that it was somewhere in the East," Sadie replied. "I think it was in New

England or up-state New York, but I can't tell you how I got that impression. Maybe it is a lingering childhood memory."

Long after the household was in darkness Nancy lay in her bed and pondered the problem of establishing Sadie's identity.

How that was to be done was not easily solved. Nancy fell asleep studying the problem, and awoke the next morning with that uppermost in her mind.

Mr. Drew took Sadie with him to the court-house for certain legal formalities, leaving Nancy alone with her mystery.

"I'll go talk with Raymond Hill," she decided. "He likes mysteries, and is probably good at solving them. Besides, he used to live in New York State, I heard him say."

It did not take Nancy long to act on an idea once she had formulated it; accordingly, she was soon in her car speeding toward Smith's Ferry, where she found Raymond Hill at his desk in the bank. The banker greeted her heartily but with genuine respect. There was nothing patronizing in his greeting; he spoke to Nancy as an equal, for she had demonstrated her courage and sagacity to his full satisfaction.

"What new twist in the mysterious doings at The Twisted Candles brings you here this morning?" Mr. Hill asked, firmly shutting the door marked "Private."

"Just a hunch," Nancy said. "Do you know where New Fernwild is?"

"New Fernwild? By jove, that sounds familiar. I have certainly heard the name often," Mr. Hill said, as a smile of hope lighted up Nancy's features. "Let me look in the government postal guide."

From his bookcase the banker took down a thick volume which, he explained, contained the name of every town and hamlet in the country, listed by states and also alphabetically.

"However, there seems to be no such place as New Fernwild listed," Mr. Hill said with a perplexed frown. "I certainly have heard or read about——"

"It is the name of an orphan asylum, Mr. Hill," Nancy said. "It may not be named after the town it is in. I guessed it might be, but if there is no such place as New Fernwild it will be harder than ever to locate the institution."

"Orphan asylum, orphan asylum," repeated Mr. Hill, running his fingers through his hair. "I have it! Goodness gracious, what a strange coincidence."

He pushed the buzzer on his desk, and to the porter who responded immediately Mr. Hill ordered that the contents of a certain safety deposit box be brought to him. While waiting for the man to return Mr. Hill drummed on the desk with his fingers, snapped them, whistled softly, and occasionally shot a searching look at Nancy under his brows. She did not break into his train of thought, although his conduct puzzled her considerably.

"Why did you come to me with this question?" Mr. Hill asked suddenly.

"The orphanage is the one from which the Semitts took Sadie," Nancy said. "I want to find out for her who her parents were. I came to you because you are interested in the case, because I suspect you like mysteries—the way you picked me out as Nancy Drew the first time I came here convinced me of that, Mr. Hill—and because you once lived in New York State where I think the orphanage is located."

"Nancy, you certainly have the best ordered mind and the keenest ability to put two and two together of any person I ever met," Mr. Hill said. "If you should decide to go into business, I'll make a place for you in the bank, and guarantee that you will be an officer in two years. I mean it. I am not joking. I think you would bring us the business of every woman in the county, and—oh, Luther, there you are!"

The porter had entered, and placed a huge bundle of legal looking documents and leather-bound account books on Mr. Hill's desk.

"Now, let's see," Mr. Hill said, assorting the papers with a practised hand. "These papers are part of the records of my father's estate. Ah, yes! I knew it."

Mr. Hill unfolded a sheaf of yellowed foolscap bound in blue paper like a lawyer's brief.

"Papers of Incorporation of the New Fern-wild Orphanage," he read. "A Charitable Institution, not operated for profit or supported by taxes, to be maintained and directed by the League for the Friendless."

"Now we are on the right track," Nancy cried, leaping to her feet in excitement. "How did it happen that you have this?"

"My father was one of the trustees of the orphanage, and president of the League for many years," Mr. Hill said. "Well, Nancy, what is to be done next?"

"How long ago was your father associated with the asylum?" Nancy asked.

"For many years, but he died twenty-two years ago."

"That is too bad," Nancy said. "Will you please do this, though, because the present management will remember who you are and will respect your wishes: Please telegraph the orphanage and ask if a little girl named Sadie Wipple was a ward there ten years ago. Ask under what circumstances she was removed."

Nancy paused a moment and Mr. Hill looked at her attentively, but when she spoke again he leaned forward and slapped the top of his desk in amazement.

"And ask," Nancy said, "if Asa Sidney, the famous inventor, was one of the contributors to the society's treasury!"

CHAPTER XX

The Clue of the Candle

Raymond Hill's eyes glowed with admiration as he arose and escorted Nancy to the door.

"I will let you know just as soon as any reply from New Fernwild arrives," he said. "I am sure you are on the right track, Nancy."

"I hope we are," Nancy replied modestly. "It is only a hunch, of course, but we must overlook no possibility."

Nancy drove directly home, and learned that her father and Sadie had not yet come back from attending to the affairs of the Sidney estate. That gave Nancy a chance to relax in a porch hammock and to read a little. She heard steps on the floor, and called out: "Is that you, Sadie?"

"Not exactly," a deep, masculine voice replied, and Nancy jumped from the hammock to confront Ned Nickerson.

"Why Ned, where in the world did you come from?" Nancy cried with sincere pleasure. "And how sunburned you are! Have you been at camp?"

"No, I have been working, believe it or not,"

the young man replied, seating himself on the porch steps and stretching his muscular arms.

"Feel that muscle, Nancy! I'll be fit as a fiddle for football when college opens again."

"Working, Ned? Where? And at what?" Nancy asked. "And can you stay for luncheon?"

"Golly, I wish I could," Ned replied, looking at Nancy with admiration. "But duty calls. In fact, I'm playing hooky this minute. I thought I'd make a stab at earning my own way this summer instead of loafing and letting Dad support me, so I got a job at High Point Inn."

"Where is that? Are you the manager, or a dish-washer?" Nancy laughed.

"Oh, nothing as responsible as either," Ned laughed back. "I drive the bus that meets all trains, carry trunks upstairs and down again, take timid, elderly ladies rowing on the river, and make myself generally useful, including pushing a lawn-mower. It's interesting, and it surely has kept me in perfect form."

"How thrilling, Ned, and how commendable!" Nancy exclaimed. "Where did you say High Point Inn is?"

"Down the river about forty miles," Ned said. "It is a rather popular, quiet sort of family resort."

"How did you get here, then?" Nancy asked. "Did you row one of the guests up?"

"Oh, nothing as strenuous as that," Ned replied. "I came up to get a couple the management just hired, a new assistant head-waiter and his wife, who comes well recommended as a pastry cook. I'll soon find out how good her recommendations are, I'll wager!"

"Are they River Heights people?" Nancy asked, her interest in the High Point Inn's new servants suddenly heightened.

"They're at a cheap boarding house down on Cadillac Street," Ned said. "Where is Cadillac Street? The number is 32, and it's called The Elite Mansion, if you can imagine that."

"Cadillac Street? You go down three blocks to the first traffic signal, and turn right three blocks down hill. It runs along the river and number 32, I judge, would be to the left," Nancy explained. "Who are these celebrated kitchen folks? French chefs?"

"Queer sort of name," Ned replied. "Cement, or something like that. Cemetery? No, Semitt. Used to have a place of their own, they said, until a crooked lawyer cheated them out of the property. There's a chance for your father to pick up some business, setting wrongs right and so forth, hey?"

"I'll mention it to him," Nancy smiled. "Must you really go?"

"I certainly must. I might lose my job," Ned said. "As long as I was in town I thought I'd take a few minutes to call and I'm glad I found you at home, Nancy. Come down to High Point

for a week-end with your father. I'll pretend I
don't know you when I carry your baggage upstairs, but I'll expect an extra large tip, though!
Goodbye, Nancy. I'll write you a postcard,
anyhow, and be sure to make no engagements
for the third week in November. Remember
the big game!''

With that farewell Ned strode off, leaped to
the seat of the trim green station-wagon he had
parked at the curb, and with a final wave he
was gone, leaving a very happy Nancy behind.

The Semitts were gone! That, indeed, was
joyful news for Sadie alone.

It was not long before Sadie and Carson
Drew drove up to the house for lunch.

"Good news, Sadie," Nancy cried, running
to meet them. "There are a dozen boxes upstairs in your room with the rest of yesterday's
purchases in them, and—the Semitts have
moved forty miles away!''

"Oh, I'm so glad," Sadie cried, while Mr.
Drew echoed her sentiments more vigorously.
Nancy explained how she had learned of the
Semitts' departure.

"Fine!" Mr. Drew said. "Sadie and I have
been to the old Twisted Candles and replaced
the court seal on the door of the Tower Room
with a stout padlock. The guards are still
there, but knowing that the Semitts are out of
the city is the best security of all.''

"I wonder if I might be permitted to prowl

around the Tower Room this afternoon, then,"
Nancy said to her father as Sadie ran upstairs
to unpack her new wardrobe.

"I think I am on the trail of Sadie's parents," Nancy explained. "There might be
some clue in the Tower Room to help me."

"Here's the key," Mr. Drew said. "Will
you explain your clues now or would you rather
wait until they develop?"

His eyes twinkled, for he knew Nancy preferred not to divulge her plans until she had
them all in working order, and as he expected
—and understood, it should be added—Nancy
said she would rather not discuss her scheme
until it produced some promise of results.

Accordingly, after luncheon Nancy and Sadie
drove off together toward the now closed tea
house. The guard at the old mansion was
dubious about permitting Nancy to enter the
locked room, although she displayed the key
and proofs of her identity.

"I don't know, Miss," the burly man said
with a shake of his head. "There's been more
than one person around trying to get into that
room. One guy said he'd gi' me a month's
wages if I let him in for just fifteen minutes."

"Well, I'm not offering any bribes," Nancy
said. "My father is the attorney for this
estate, as I told you, and this young woman is
the owner. What did the persons look like who
tried to enter?"

At the man's description of the two men who had at various times sought entrance to Asa Sidney's study, Nancy and Sadie exchanged glances.

"Peter Boonton!"

"And Jacob Sidney!"

"You know 'em, then?" the guard asked.

"We do indeed, and I shall commend you to my father for not accepting the bribes," Nancy said warmly. "You will lose nothing by being honest."

Greatly mollified, the guard hemmed and hawed, and then said he would permit Nancy to enter the room if Sadie would remain outside as a guarantee of good faith, and if Nancy would promise to lock the door behind her.

"How can I, with a padlock?" Nancy asked.

"Oh, Mr. Drew put a hasp on the inside of the door, too," Sadie said. "He locked the door behind him when we were up here this morning."

"Are you the young lady who was here with Mr. Drew today?" the guard asked with a greater show of confidence. "My partner told me about it when I relieved him on this post at noon. Sure, you can go up, ladies."

"I'll stay down, anyhow," Sadie said. "It would make me feel too sad to see the room again so soon after Mr. Sidney's death."

Nancy mounted the familiar stairs by herself, unlocked the heavy padlock, and entered the musty, stuffy Tower Room which needed airing badly. She locked the door behind her and then paused to survey the room.

"What is it about the room that seems so unusual?" she asked herself. "Oh, I know. All the candles standing around in it, and some of them in such odd places."

Like a good general, Nancy sat down to plan her campaign before beginning any action.

"Those oddly-twisted candles certainly are in queer nooks," she mused. "I wonder if that is significant of anything."

On the mantelshelf of the fireplace stood two handsome, stately candles in silver holders.

"I believe those pieces," thought the speculating girl, "will bring real money as valuable antiques some day."

She placed a chair before the yawning opening of the fireplace and climbed upon its rush-bottomed seat. Carefully she fingered the heavy pieces as she stood up closely to survey the beautiful objects.

"I wonder," she mused as she lightly touched the shelf, "if a brick below this holder isn't a bit uneven."

Nancy rather thought the stone tilted as she replaced the holder onto the shelf. Cautiously stepping off the old chair she pushed it to the opposite end of the shelf where the twin candles stood. The light from the window fell directly on the shelf at this point.

"I do see something different up here," muttered the girl. "It's another loose brick at this end."

At once Nancy set to work to pry up the loosened bricks. It was a tedious task and several times the low chair threatened to tip perilously, but the determined girl stuck to her job.

"I must help Sadie to find the hidden valuables, and if each candle mark is, as I think, a treasure spot, it will be easy."

She drew forth a tightly-rolled package heavily bound with a leather thong. Quickly she stepped off the chair and laid the heavy package down on it, then untied the fastening. Revealed were twenty-dollar gold pieces neatly wrapped in single packages of one hundred dollars each. At the opposite end of the shelf was a similar bundle. The girl opened that one also.

"Three thousand dollars!" calculated Nancy rapidly. "How remarkable! Mr. Sidney was a queer but lovable old man. Now I know how to reveal more of his precious secrets for Sadie."

Hastily the young detective put the gold packages back into their hiding places, lest someone enter and guess her plan. Nancy turned toward the tower window, still hoping to find a clue pertaining to the parentage of the faithful young heiress.

She walked slowly toward the massive, carved desk-table that filled the space below the center window, on which stood the biggest twisted candle of all. The candle stood on a battered old Bible which Nancy reverently moved to one side. The place where it had rested on the wood was brighter and dust-free compared with the rest of the surface, but within the border of the exposed area her sharp eyes detected a hair-like crack. Tracing the outline of the almost invisible line, Nancy saw that it marked an oblong about a foot wide and fourteen or fifteen inches in length.

"A secret compartment!" she exclaimed aloud. "Now, how to open it?"

Her fingers searched the surface of the table for a spring which might release the lid of the secret compartment, but to no avail. At length, however, her patient and minute search was rewarded, when she found a slight indentation on the under side of the projecting edge of the table-top.

At the pressure of her fingers the secret compartment flew open, revealing a recess about six inches deep. Nancy peered inside and saw an orderly pile of papers. Should she examine them, or would it be a better plan, considering the legal tangles, to have her father take them from the secret compartment in the presence of witnesses and look at the documents?

"I think I'll leave it," she decided, firmly

shutting the lid of the hidden recess and pushing the Bible back over the place.

The ancient and well-worn book, to Nancy's great distress, fell into two parts as she lifted it, and several loose pages dropped to the floor. She carefully gathered them up and opened the volume to replace them in their proper order. As she turned the pages she suddenly came upon a letter, and the printed address in the upper left-hand corner made her stand as if transfixed.

It was from the New Fernwild Orphanage!

What would its contents reveal? Was her search already at an end?

Nancy's hand trembled as she reached for the letter, which she saw was addressed in pen and ink to Asa Sidney. The stamp was of a pattern now discontinued, although the date on the cancellation mark was blurred so as to be indecipherable.

Suddenly a sharp rap on the door startled Nancy. She jumped back, permitting the cover of the Bible to fall into place, thereby concealing the letter.

"Who is there?" she asked.

"It's I, Nancy, Sadie," came a familiar voice through the stout panels, and Nancy quickly unlocked the door to permit her friend to enter. She carefully replaced the padlock and snapped it shut.

"It—it looks just as Mr. Sidney left it,"

Sadie said, surveying the room through eyes brimming with tears.

"It is what he left that interests me," Nancy said. "Sadie, I hope to have more good news for you. First let me explain why I came here to look around. I was so intent on my theory I never stopped to consider that you might think me impudent to go poking around in your property while you are locked out."

"Why, Nancy dear, I never dreamed—I wouldn't think of—Nancy!"

Sadie was incoherent in her efforts to tell Nancy how grateful she was for all that had been done for her, and Nancy smiled happily at the evidence of Sadie's trust and affection.

"Hush, Sadie! Listen to me now," she said. "I have asked Mr. Hill——"

"Mr. Hill!" Sadie exclaimed, leaping to her feet. "I came up to tell you about Mr. Hill! He just telephoned here. He called up the house and Hannah told him we were here. He wants you to come to see him at once, and he wants to see me, too."

"Good!" Nancy cried. "He must have an answer from New Fernwild."

Sadie looked bewildered, and Nancy hastened to explain.

"With Mr. Hill's help I located the orphanage, and he surprised me by telling me that his father had been trustee of the place years ago. I asked him to telegraph there to find out about you, and to find out if Mr. Sidney had been interested in the asylum while you were sheltered there.''

''Why in the world?'' Sadie asked.

''Sadie, I think—I can't prove anything yet, but I believe there is proof within arm's length of me now, if Mr. Hill hasn't it already, that Mr. Sidney left you his fortune because you are his rightful heir!''

Sadie leaned back in her seat, her face white.

''D-do you me-mean that I—'' she began.

''I mean that I believe you are related to him,'' Nancy said. ''And now, in this old Bible——''

At that moment a frightful howl echoed through the old house, followed by a reverberating crash!

CHAPTER XXI

MISSING!

CARSON DREW was dictating letters. Much important work had been neglected by his absorption in Sadie's case, and he was trying to catch up with his correspondence after seeing Nancy and Sadie off on their quest at the old house.

High in River Heights's most important office building was Mr. Drew's office, and as he dictated to his efficient secretary his eyes wandered over the rolling hills that met the river.

A knock at the door of the outer office did not interrupt Mr. Drew. He had given orders to his staff that he should not be disturbed.

"Excuse me, Mr. Drew," the office boy said, hesitatingly poking his head into the private office. "Excuse me, but Mr. Cochran is outside and he says he has to talk to you."

"Mr. Cochran? Show him in at once," Carson Drew exclaimed. "That will do, Miss Farley. I'll call you when I wish to continue."

Mr. Drew awaited Mr. Cochran's entrance with interest, because he was the lawyer retained by the disappointed heirs to break Asa

Sidney's will and to deprive Sadie of her inheritance.

"Sit down, Mr. Cochran," Carson Drew said pleasantly.

"Thanks! I hope you'll excuse me for insisting upon seeing you. As a lawyer you will realize that this visit is rather unusual. We are opponents, technically speaking," Mr. Cochran began.

"An unusual case," was Mr. Drew's guarded comment.

"Unusual? If you say it is unusual from your side, I wonder what you would think of it if you were in my position," the visiting lawyer said with a wry smile. "Mind you, I think a good case could be made out for the practically disinherited relatives, but I really don't relish the job very much. The people I represent are so suspicious of each other that I begin to suspect the sincerity of their claims against your client. That is speaking very frankly."

"It is," Mr. Drew smiled. "I suppose you will attempt to prove, if this case comes to court, that Mr. Sidney was not in his right mind and was unduly influenced by Miss Wipple to the extent that he left his fortune to the orphan waitress, and his loving relatives were cheated."

Cochran smiled wryly.

"I realized fully that a lawyer of your experience would anticipate the tactics of the opposition," he said formally. "That, of course, is what the plaintiffs wish to have proven.

"Now, I have come to make you a proposition, Mr. Drew. It would save your client unpleasant notoriety if this case were settled out of court. Can't we come to some agreement?"

"I don't think so," Mr. Drew said quietly. "Miss Wipple's case is a just and honest one, or else I would not be representing her. We are prepared to contest the unfair claims of the Boontons and the Sidneys, and there can be no compromise."

"Well, I have done my duty," Cochran said. "Now, speaking as man to man and not as lawyer to lawyer, I must confess I wish I hadn't taken the case. Whether their claims are good or weak, my clients scarcely inspire me to enter the lists for them with any great enthusiasm."

"Then, if I were in your position, I should withdraw," Mr. Drew said tersely.

"I don't want to be called a quitter," Cochran said. "Besides, I think my clients are legally right, even if they are not very pleasant and agreeable."

The two lawyers arose as Cochran prepared to depart. They turned their heads toward the outer office as the sounds of heated argument came to them through the doors.

"What can that be?" Mr. Drew asked, pressing a bell-button to summon his secretary.

"They are Mr. Sidney and Mr. Boonton," she reported, and with that the door burst open and the two men named came into the office.

"This is rather an intrusion," Mr. Drew said, confronting the excited cousins across his desk.

"That's all right," Boonton replied. "I am not going to be cheated out of my just rights. I saw Jacob come into the building and I followed him just to see what he was up to. And he comes here to the office of the attorney for the fortune-hunting Sadie! And who else is here? Geoffrey Cochran, the lawyer I was led to hire to protect my interests and that of my niece. It looks funny!"

"Be quiet!" Boonton roared. "I was getting a hair-cut across the street when I saw Cochran rush in here, so I came on up to Drew's office on a hunch."

"What do you mean, anyhow?" Cochran asked. "I came up to ask Mr. Drew if he would consider a settlement out of court."

"Well, I hope Drew turned you down," Jacob Sidney fumed. "Our case is good. We don't have to be afraid of any money-seeking waitress. We hired you because we heard you were good at breaking down witnesses, not because you were good at dodging work."

Cochran's face flushed, and he slammed Mr. Drew's desk with his fist.

"That settles it," he thundered. "I refuse to take your case. I resign as your lawyer, and it gives me exceedingly great satisfaction to do so."

"You were never with us," Jacob Sidney sneered. "We'll get ourselves another lawyer, and we'll carry the case to the highest court in the land before we give up. Sadie Wipple won't have a cent of her stolen money left when we get through, and what's more, she'll be in prison!"

"I can't permit this vulgar quarreling in my office!" Mr. Drew shouted. "Please leave at once!"

"Yes, get out of here," Cochran seconded. "You couldn't send Miss Wipple to jail, even if you won your case."

"Oh, maybe you think we can't send Sadie to jail, hey?" Peter Boonton snapped. "Don't be so sure of that. We've talked this over and the whole business looks pretty bad to us, pretty bad!"

"Stop! What do you mean?" Mr. Drew demanded, striding across the room and placing his back against the door.

Boonton and Sidney, suspicious of each other as they were, drew close together and confronted the angry lawyers.

"I'll tell you what he means," Jacob snarled, his face flushed with rage. "He means that it is a mighty queer thing, that right after a

visit to old Asa by two young ladies, mentioning no names, he makes his will all of a sudden
in favor of one of them and then dies the next
day—and the lady who finds him dead is the
one that gets his money. If that's not——"

"That is the most infamous accusation I
ever listened to," Mr. Drew exclaimed. "Let
me warn you that it is you who will be in jail
for spreading such base scandal!"

"And let me add to that, Sirs," Cochran
shouted, "that not only do I refuse to handle
your case, but I hereby offer my full services
to Miss Wipple and Miss Drew."

What further argument might have taken
place was never revealed, because Miss Farley
again pushed the door open.

"Excuse me, Mr. Drew, but your housekeeper is on the wire and she insists upon talking with you," the secretary said.

"Why, it is getting close to dinner time,"
Mr. Drew said, glancing at his watch. "I'll
speak to her at once."

He lifted the receiver of his private telephone, and as he listened his face grew grave,
then decidedly apprehensive. Putting the instrument down, he turned to Cochran.

"My daughter and Miss Wipple are *missing*," he said hoarsely. "They were supposed
to have gone to the old house and then to Raymond Hill's office. They cannot be located at
either place!"

CHAPTER XXII

A Rascally Ruse

The ear-piercing yell so startled Nancy and Sadie that they forgot for the moment the exciting theory which Nancy had just told to Sadie.

"Wha-what was that?" Sadie chattered. "It sounded like a ghost!"

"Stuff and nonsense," Nancy cried, running to the window, and struggling with the stiff, warped old sash.

Sadie ran to the door first and then returned to Nancy's side, as much for the assurance of being close to that self-possessed young woman as of aiding her. Between them the girls raised the window and Nancy peered out.

"Goodness, there is a man on the porch roof with a ladder on top of him," she exclaimed. "How did he get there? He looks badly hurt."

Sadie took her turn at the window.

"It isn't the guard," she said. "Where can he be?"

"Let us run down and see," Nancy proposed. "We must find out who the man is, and do something for him."

180

She ran to the door and unlocked it, and as
carefully padlocked it behind her before start-
ing down the stairs to the second floor. Sadie
followed close behind, and the two girls made
their way to a front room, the windows of
which opened out upon the roof of the porch
where the mysterious man lay groaning beneath
the ladder.

It was a struggle to raise the sash, but at
last Nancy was able to climb out upon the roof.
She tugged the heavy ladder from the prostrate
man, and tenderly rolled him on his back.

"Frank Semitt!" Nancy cried.

"Oh, he has come after me," Sadie wailed.

"He doesn't look as if he were able to do
anyone much harm," Nancy said, putting her
fingers on the unconscious man's wrist. At her
touch Semitt stirred and groaned hollowly.

"Where am I?" he moaned. "Oh, my poor
head, my poor back."

"You are where you certainly don't belong,"
Nancy said, steeling her heart against the pity
she felt for the obviously suffering Semitt.

"Oh, I'm terribly hurt. I think I am dying,"
Semitt moaned, rolling his eyes back.

"Sadie, help me carry him inside," Nancy
said. "We can't let him lie here. Where is
that guard?"

With great difficulty the two girls slowly and
carefully carried Semitt, who seemed to have
lapsed into semiconsciousness, over to the bed-

room window. Nancy crept into the room and then took Semitt's shoulders and half lifted, half dragged him across the sill. Sadie did her best to assist, but her frail strength did not lend much aid. It was impossible to lift Semitt to the bed, so Nancy placed a pillow under his head and another under his back.

"Oh, oh," Semitt groaned. "Where—oh, I remember now. Sadie, where is my dear little Sadie, whom I love so much?"

"Before we go into that, Mr. Semitt, what were you doing with the ladder on the porch roof?" Nancy asked. She had knelt beside Semitt and again put her fingers on his pulse. The pulse count showed her that the man's heart was beating a little more rapidly than is normal. It was not, as was to be expected if he were badly hurt, beating slowly and irregularly. Nancy began to suspect that Semitt was pretending.

"There are some of my own belongings in the house, things I value and which the law won't let me get in to find," Semitt said. "There's a picture of Sadie when she was a little tot, and a lock of her hair, and her first arithmetic paper with a big red A on it, and——"

"Oh, do tell the truth!" Nancy cried. "You can't convince me that you would risk your life and a prison sentence for burglary to get a lock of hair and a snapshot."

"Oh, oh, you misjudge me cruelly," Semitt sighed. "Sadie, come to your poor father, who is stricken to death just for love of you."

That was such flagrant fraud that Nancy stood up and scanned the prostrate Semitt with scorn.

"I don't think you are hurt at all," she said. "Your cheeks are pink, your pulse is normal, and your speech is pure hypocrisy!"

The suspicion was now firmly established in her mind that Semitt had tried to enter the house to search for further loot, and had failed because all entrances were firmly locked and the guard alone had the key to the front door, which he himself was not supposed to enter.

Had he really fallen, Nancy wondered. And was he trying to make minor injuries appear to be serious ones in an effort to win Sadie's sympathy? Or was it possible that it was all a ruse to gain admittance to the house? If so, where was the guard? Was he, perhaps, an accomplice of Semitt?

The inn-keeper's eyes closed once more and his lips moved soundlessly.

"Speak up," Nancy said, more sharply than she really felt. "I can't hear you."

The man beckoned to Nancy to place her ears closer so she could hear. She would not do it.

Nancy's suspicions, of course, were entirely correct. Semitt had seen the girls arrive at the former inn, and from his ladder he had watched them in the Tower Room. All entrance to the place was barred to him and he had realized that the only way to gain admittance was by means of a trick. He had carefully posed himself under the ladder, then drummed with his heels on the tin roof, screaming to simulate an accident.

And now, he thought bitterly as he lay playing 'possum, that sharp-eyed Nancy Drew was seeing through his sham! She would not even lean over him to hear what he was saying, would she?

Semitt suddenly sat bolt upright, and with a sweep of his arms threw Nancy off her balance. She reeled and fell against Sadie, and in a flash Semitt had whipped a sheet from the bed and was looping it over the heads and arms of the surprised girls.

Nancy fought like a tigress, blinded and bound as she was; she kicked and she screamed. Sadie, frightened to speechlessness, only got in Nancy's way.

Something wet and very, very cold drenched Nancy's face; something that smelled pungently. She held her breath and closed her eyes against the stinging fumes. A sleeping potion —she was being drugged!

Fight as she would, Nancy could not hold her breath indefinitely. Her tortured lungs seemed to be bursting and she was forced to inhale deeply. The floor seemed to be giving way beneath her feet. Down—down, on great invisible wings. Down—down——

Sometime later Nancy opened her eyes and breathed deeply again. What had happened? She was stretched on the floor of the bedroom, alone. It was dusk outside. And her head ached violently.

"Sadie!"

There was no answer.

Nancy pulled herself to her feet, and clinging to the wall for support groped her way out of the room into the darker hall, and step by step down the stairs. The key was still in the front door where Sadie had left it after obtaining it from the guard to answer the telephone.

With infinite effort Nancy turned the key and staggered out upon the porch. The fresh, cool air revived her a great deal, but she had to sit down on the steps to gather her dazed wits.

Where was Sadie? Nancy reproached herself bitterly for having fallen into the wily Semitt's trap.

Refreshed at last, she arose and looked for her car. It was gone. Semitt had evidently taken it—and Sadie, too.

"I'll telephone home," she cried aloud. "Oh, if only I am not too late!"

As she turned to reënter the house, Nancy was taken aback at the sight of a pair of large feet in thick-soled shoes protruding from beneath the steps of the house.

CHAPTER XXIII

The Kidnaped Heiress

A more timid person than Nancy Drew would have fled in fear and horror from the scene. To Nancy, however, the motionless, half-concealed limbs meant that someone was in distress, and that meant more to her than her own immediate safety.

She seized the man's ankles. Although the effects of the drug had left her still weak and dizzy, she tugged until she had pulled the unconscious person into full view.

"It's the watchman!" she exclaimed, kneeling beside the still form and raising the man's head to her lap.

The guard groaned and his eyelids fluttered. Immediately Nancy rolled the man over, turned his head to one side, and began to administer artificial respiration. As clean, fresh air replaced the fumes of the sleeping potion in his lungs the man began to stir.

Suddenly tires crunched on the gravel of the driveway and the beams of twin headlights cut through the twilight, falling full upon the laboring girl and the man she was striving to rescue.

A shout, and the squealing of brakes suddenly applied, made Nancy leap to her feet, certain that Semitt had returned to finish his criminal plot.

"Nancy! What is the matter? Are you hurt?"

"Dad!" Nancy cried, recognizing first the voice and then the form of the man who leaped from the car. "Oh, Dad! We were trapped by Frank Semitt. He drugged the watchman and me, and has fled with Sadie!"

"Great Scott!" Carson Drew exclaimed, folding Nancy in his arms. "Hill, did you hear?"

Raymond Hill emerged from the car just as the watchman sat up, blinking in the glare of the headlights.

"This is bad business," the banker said. "It is a matter for the police."

"What happened to me?" the guard asked thickly. "Did you knock me down with the car you were driving?"

"No, you were drugged," Nancy said.

"I remember everything now," the man said, struggling to his feet. "A fellow came and said he was a servant of Mr. Drew and had come to help the girls. I wouldn't let him in, so he showed me some cards and papers to prove he had a right to enter. When I leaned over to look at them he clapped a cloth soaked in some drug over my mouth and nose. That's all I remember."

In as few words as possible Nancy told what had happened to her and, as far as she could, to Sadie.

"There is no time to be lost," Mr. Drew agreed. "Watchman, suppose you go to the old farmhouse where the other man is and find out if anybody was near that place. We must get after the Semitts, but the question is, where did they go?"

"Let us drive to High Point Inn, where Ned Nickerson said they had taken up employment today," Nancy suggested.

It was agreed that was the best clue. Accordingly, Mr. Hill, Nancy, and Carson Drew jumped into the latter's automobile and sped off for the river resort.

It was a long drive, and few words were exchanged on the journey. Nancy's mind was busy trying to fit together the scant clues and her reasons of the motives for the kidnaping. What had the Semitts to gain by the daring crime? Did they intend to hold Sadie for ransom? If so, where had they taken the girl?

At last the gayly-illuminated grounds of High Point Inn came into view. Electrically-lit Japanese lanterns were strung between the trees like giant flowers from another world. The great porches were crowded with gay couples—men in white flannels and women and girls in airy summer frocks. Music from an orchestra hidden behind a grove of evergreens added to the

joyous atmosphere of the place, and a search-
light sweeping over the river revealed row-
boats and canoes drifting about with their
happy occupants.

The gayety of the scene was lost on Nancy.
Grim business had to be done. She leaped from
the car before it came to a halt and ran to the
entrance of the hotel without pausing to return
the puzzled looks of the vacationists she passed.

"I want to see the manager at once," Nancy
told the clerk at the desk.

"No more rooms," the clerk said. "It won't
do any good to see the manager."

"I don't want rooms," Nancy said. "Let
me talk with him at once, please. It is a matter
of life or death."

The clerk's eyes protruded from his head.
He summoned a bellboy at once and sent him
off to find a Mr. Harmon. Just as Mr. Hill and
Mr. Drew entered the lobby, Mr. Harmon, a fat,
jolly man in evening dress, stepped up to
Nancy.

"I'll explain later," Nancy said to him.
"First, tell me if you employed a couple named
Semitt today or yesterday."

"I did, but they did not stay long," Mr.
Harmon said. "Their references were not
satisfactory."

Mr. Drew introduced himself and Mr. Hill
to the proprietor, briefly explaining why Nancy
was so concerned about the Semitts.

"They left about three o'clock," Mr. Harmon said. "They drove down in their own machine."

"Their own car?" asked Nancy in surprise. "I heard they were brought here by a friend of mine who is working here."

"Well, young Nickerson went to their boarding place, but the Semitts were very haughty and said they'd prefer coming in their own car. Now they've gone, and where they went to I don't know."

"Then the next clue is their old address," Nancy said, looking around in the hope of catching sight of Ned Nickerson. That young man was not to be seen, and Nancy regretfully concluded that there was no time to hunt him up, and nothing to be gained by it, anyhow.

"Ned said they were boarding at a place called the Magnificent Mansion, or something like that, in Cadillac Street, River Heights," Nancy told her father. "Let us go there."

After thanking the manager of the inn briefly the three hurried out, and Mr. Drew pointed the car toward the city.

"I remember the name of the boarding house now," Nancy said. "The Elite Mansion is the place and the number is 32 Cadillac Street."

"Do you think they would go back there?" Mr. Hill asked doubtfully.

"No, I don't," Nancy said. "We may, however, find some stray bit of information which

would give us a hint as to where they would
most likely go. A letter from some other town
or state, a sentence overheard by the boarding
house mistress—who can tell?''

The car sped past the Drew home without
stopping, and turned into Cadillac Street, a bare
and ordinary looking thoroughfare where ware-
houses and docks lined one side and small shops
and cheap rooming houses the other.

The appearance of the street improved
toward its head. A third-rate boat club and the
piers of the excursion steamers replaced the
dingier docks on the river side, while opposite
them a row of houses that had once been occupied by prosperous river captains gave the
street an air of decayed respectability. Number 32 was one of these shabby old homes.

Again Nancy was the first one up the steps.
A slatternly colored maid answered the bell,
and when Nancy asked for the Semitts the
servant said bluntly that they were not at home.

''Then let me speak to the proprietor, and
quickly, too,'' Nancy commanded. ''This is a
matter of the law, and I am not responsible for
what will happen to anybody who delays me.''

''I think, Hill,'' Mr. Drew said with a laugh
to his companion at the foot of the front steps,
''that we will let Nancy conduct this investigation without interference. She seems to know
what she is about.''

The boarding house mistress, a huge woman

with hair of a vivid, metallic yellow, who was dressed in a much-beruffled gown of purple organdie, hurried to the door.

"What is the matter, dearie?" she asked, looking at Nancy with hard eyes. "What's this my Daisy tells me about getting the law chased onto her?"

"I am looking for a couple named Semitt— Frank and Emma Semitt," Nancy replied, smiling pleasantly. "I'm sorry if I frightened your maid, but I must have the information quickly. It concerns an inheritance."

Nancy calculated that a tempting hint such as a mention of an inheritance would make the woman more voluble, and her appraisal of Queenie Dilberry was not wrong.

"An inheritance? Fancy that, now. Isn't that exciting!" Mrs. Dilberry cried. "Honey, I'd give my right arm to help you, but Frank and Emma went away this noon. A lovely couple. I wish they could have stayed forever. So refined!"

"No doubt," Nancy said dryly. "Where did they go?"

"They took a job at a swell hotel up the river," Mrs. Dilberry said. "Took all their stuff. Car and all."

"They left the hotel at once," Nancy said. "I was just there. They—they didn't take the position. I wonder if you have any idea where they might have gone?"

"Dearie, I ain't got the slightest!" Mrs. Dilberry said earnestly. "They didn't seem to have friends, and they didn't get no mail during the time that they was here. Ain't that a shame, now!"

"Yes, a big shame," Nancy said disappointedly. "I would willingly give fifty dollars for information that would locate them."

The boarding house mistress's eyes popped at the size of the reward, but it was plainly evident that she was honestly ignorant as to the Semitts' whereabouts.

"Thank you, at any rate," Nancy said. "I shan't waste any more of your time."

She then rejoined her father and Mr. Hill.

"Where next, Nancy?" Mr. Drew asked.

"We might stop off at the house on the chance that Sadie was brought home, or that the Semitts called up to arrange for a ransom," Nancy suggested.

However, nothing had been heard of Sadie by telephone or any other means.

"This is certainly a matter for the police, then," Mr. Drew said. "Nancy, you must be exhausted after your trying experiences. You must stay here and let Hannah fix you a warm bath and a light supper. Mr. Hill and I will get the state troopers and private detectives busy at once."

"Dad, please," Nancy begged. "I am hungry—I did not know it until this minute. I shall feel better after a bite to eat, but I must go with you. I should be worried to death doing nothing at home, while Sadie——"

Hannah, at the mention of food, had trotted into the kitchen and returned with a bowl of rich chicken broth which she had kept warm all evening.

"Here, Nancy dear, eat it right off the library table," she said. "I'll bring you some milk and crackers. And you, Mr. Drew, and the gentleman——?"

"We bought some frankfurters at Smith's Ferry," Mr. Drew smiled. "They spoiled my appetite."

"And mine," Mr. Hill added. "Thank you, but I know I couldn't eat a mouthful, Mrs. Gruen."

As Nancy sipped her liquid supper she pondered the situation. Where could the Semitts have vanished?

"I've finished," she said suddenly, putting down her glass. "Let's go back to The Twisted Candles."

"Why?"

"The Twisted Candles!"

The two men could not believe their ears.

"Yes, the old house itself," Nancy said. "I am sure that is where we shall find the answer to the whole riddle. Oh, the more I think of it the more I am sure I am right."

CHAPTER XXIV

THE GLEAM IN THE DARK

NANCY DREW sat alone in the back seat of the speeding car that raced once more over the now familiar road to the old Sidney home. Her mind, too, was racing. Her decision to return to The Sign of the Twisted Candles had been made "on a hunch," as she would have explained it, but it must be remembered that her successful hunches were always the result of constructive thinking.

This had been Nancy's train of thought as she had sipped her milk. Whatever it was that Frank Semitt was after, whether actual treasure or just valuable information, it was certainly in the old house. About that there was no question.

Sadie had been kidnaped from the house and the Semitts had vanished. Where would the pursuers be least likely to search for them?

"The scene of the kidnaping, of course," had flashed into Nancy's mind. "Nobody, Frank Semitt will reason, would look for him or for Sadie at the place from which he stole the girl!"

"Don't you think you better cut off your

motor and just coast up to the house?'' Nancy advised her father. ''Put out the lights, too.''

''Here goes, then,'' Mr. Drew replied, switching off the headlights and throwing his gears into neutral.

The car rolled silently up to the big old house, dark and almost invisible against its background of trees. Nancy felt a pang of disappointment. The place looked as deserted as if no living person had been near the mansion for years.

''Let us make a circuit of the house first and see if we can find the watchman,'' Nancy whispered. Noiselessly she stole along on the grass, the two men following her closely.

Slowly she led the way around The Twisted Candles. As she turned the corner of the kitchen wing Nancy sniffed the air. Someone had recently been smoking a pipe close by!

She put out a hand to halt the men behind her, and hugging the walls closely she slipped around the end of the house. A low murmur of voices came to Nancy's alert ears!

''Who is there?'' she called softly.

Instantly the conversation ceased. Nancy waited breathlessly for a moment and then advanced boldly toward the source of the now hushed sounds. If the watchmen were conferring, they would be less apt to shoot if Nancy made a bold move than if she skulked in the shadows. If the speakers should be the

Semitts, she had Mr. Drew and Mr. Hill close behind to aid her.

"Who is that?" came growlingly out of the dark.

"Nancy Drew," replied the girl. "And you?"

"We were wondering where you were," came the unexpected reply. "This is Peter Boonton. Jacob Sidney's here, too."

Nancy turned and called to her father and Mr. Hill to come closer.

"Boonton and Sidney are here," she said under her breath.

The two groups met at the back steps of the house, each demanding of the other reasons for the mysterious visit in the dark.

"Jacob and I met uptown and started to argue," Peter Boonton said. "I don't know just why we drove down here. I'll admit I've been here before, but the watchman never let me get onto the lawn, even. Tonight he isn't to be seen anywhere."

"What's that! The watchman gone?" Mr. Drew asked.

"We haven't seen him, anyhow," Peter Boonton said. "Don't think we've broken into the place, or even tried to. I'm getting sick and tired of trying to outsmart this young lady here. And when we found her car in the shed over there, why, we just decided to sit down and see what she was up to now."

"Oh, my car is in the shed, is it?" Nancy

asked with decided interest. "That's news, because it was stolen from here this afternoon."

"Who stole it, do you think?" Jacob asked. "You can be sure we didn't."

"Frank Semitt took it, after he drugged the watchman and me and kidnaped Sadie," Nancy said bluntly. "And that is what we are doing here—looking for Sadie."

"What! Semitt did that? Why should he want to kidnap Sadie?" the cousins demanded.

"Probably to get his hands on Asa Sidney's hidden wealth," Nancy said. "He has been looting this place systematically. We recovered valuable silver and rare old linens, besides bonds as good as gold that he had secreted. That is the kind of partner you had in your attempts to deprive Sadie of her inheritance!"

"I told you we shouldn't have taken Semitt in with us," Jacob accused Peter. "I never trusted him."

"Yes, he was just using us to his own advantage," Peter said gloomily. "And now he has turned kidnaper and car thief, too."

"And you fall into such company all on account of a silly, fifty-year-old family feud which never affected either one of you," Nancy said pointedly. "Thank goodness, I have convinced George and Bess that they must not be as silly as their elders and warp their lives with borrowed hatred!"

"Yes, Bess and George told me they made up

with you," Peter Boonton replied. "I was mad at first, but I got over it. It does seem sort of foolish. Old Asa never in the world would have willingly caused his baby's death. His wife was mean to leave him."

"That's what we Sidneys have always said," Jacob commented.

"Yes, but what did you Sidneys do? You treated every Boonton like a mad dog," Peter retorted.

"It does sound ridiculous when you talk it over," Nancy interjected. "And now it has resulted in danger of the worst sort to Sadie—this childish quarreling and greedy claim on the estate!"

"Honestly, I feel so disgusted with it all I can't even get up enough dignity to feel mad at being scolded by a chit of a girl," Boonton sighed. "Jacob, you are an old fool and I am another."

"Maybe even a couple of old fools can help find poor Sadie," Jacob replied. "What's to be done?"

"My idea is to notify the police and have a state-wide alarm sent out," Mr. Hill said.

"Yes, but what about the watchman?" Mr. Drew asked. "And what was Nancy's idea in coming here? She had a plan of some kind. Nancy! Where are you?"

Nancy, however, had slipped away from the group. So her car had been hidden in the shed!

Had Semitt come back to The Sign of the Twisted Candles in her car or had he hidden it that afternoon?

She continued her examination of the grounds, step by step. There was no sign of the watchman at all, and Nancy recalled with a shudder, as she completed the circuit of the building and reached the front steps again, the shock of discovering the drugged man at that self-same spot.

Silently the girl contemplated the building. Her eyes swept up and down the sprawling contours. What a story the old house could tell if it could speak. What a——

"Is that a light?" she suddenly asked herself.

Upstairs in the tower the windows seemed to show a lesser degree of darkness than the blank panes elsewhere in the house. Was it a reflection of the stars, or was it some faint inner glow that made them appear so different?

Nancy looked more sharply.

"It seems as if the windows have been covered so a light won't show through," she said to herself. "That certainly looks like a crack of light at the bottom of the middle window, or else my eyes are playing tricks!"

She started for the front door, and then recalled the ladder still lying on the porch roof, where Semitt had played his trick upon her.

Flanking the porch steps on either side were

stout lattices built of age-enduring locust wood,
up which honey-suckle and cinnamon vine clam-
bered. Nancy reached through the foliage and
gripped the sturdy wooden support. Her toes
found a foothold, and with an ease that surprised even herself she was soon over the edge
of the porch roof. Heedless of rust and dirt
she climbed over the edge and drew herself
erect.

Yes, there was the ladder! It was slow work
to handle the heavy contraption without making
a sound, but Nancy managed at last to rest the
top rung against the sill of the center tower
window, without the least tell-tale scrape or
rattle.

She tested the ladder. It was not a very
sturdy affair, because one leg was shorter than
the other. However, Nancy figured that by
keeping her weight to one side, she would be
able to keep the ladder balanced.

Rung by rung, with infinite caution, Nancy
mounted toward the tower windows. The ladder gave a sickening lurch as she came close to
the top, and the daring girl reached out and
clung to the dusty sill of the window just above
her head.

She did not dare look upward for fear of losing her balance. With most of her weight supported by her hands Nancy continued her climb.
Two steps more, and she was able to put her
forearm on the sill and curl her fingers around

the iron peg that held the shutters when they were closed. Cautiously she raised her head until her eyes were on a level with the window frame.

She was standing now on the top rung of the ladder, a precarious position but a triumphant one! It was plain that the windows had been draped with some sort of heavy cloth to exclude the light that was burning within, because Nancy could clearly detect the candle glow through the tiny pin-prick apertures in the cloth. More than that, her sharp ears heard the low rumble in the room of a masculine voice.

Cautious still, and taking infinite pains to retain her balance, Nancy thrust her fingers under the edge of the window and sought to lift it. She was rewarded as the frame moved upward half an inch, then an inch, and yet another half. Then the frame gave a tiny squeak and seemed to stick, and for a breathless moment Nancy ducked her head and waited for detection.

However, the voice droned on without interruption, and Nancy again dared to raise her eyes to the level of the sill. The cloth had evidently been fastened to the inner frame, not to the window sash, because the gap she had made by raising the window was still covered.

Though Nancy could make no use of her eyes in gathering information about what was going on in the Tower Room, she could still make good use of her sense of hearing. She realized that the voice was—Frank Semitt's. Nancy had known it would prove to be his.

"—you and that Drew girl spent the whole day up here. I'm sure you know where the stuff is. Old Asa had plenty. Where is it? Don't sniffle. You won't ever see Nancy again, anyhow, so you might as well tell. If you'll let us see where the stuff is, or where you and she hid it, you'll get your share. If you don't tell, you'll have to come with us anyhow, and you'll have to work hard for a living 'cause we ain't got anything, see? You like them pretty clothes you got on, don't you? Come on and tell! I'll give you one minute more, and then you'll get another taste of the whip!"

The brutal voice droned on and on and on, and through it all Nancy could hear the quiet weeping of Sadie.

"I tell you I know nothing," the orphan choked.

"Forty seconds more, and then the whip again," Mrs. Semitt chimed in. "Thirty-five seconds."

"And what's more, if you won't tell us we'll get Nancy Drew as easy as we got you," Semitt said. "We'll set a trap for her because we'll make you write a note to her to come to see you. Then you can watch us force her to tell where the gold is!"

"Oh, don't, please," Sadie wept. "I'll work

for you, do anything for you, but don't **harm** Nancy.''

"Time's up," Mrs. Semitt said.

Nancy, shaken with horror at Sadie's torture, lifted the cloth that hung over the window. She peered in on a dramatic tableau.

Sadie, her pretty new frock rumpled **and** stained, one sleeve all but ripped off and her hair in disarray, stood leaning against the old table-desk with the secret drawer not three feet from Nancy. Her face was turned in profile, staring toward Frank Semitt and his wife. Mrs. Semitt stood with arms folded, an evil smile on her face, while her husband was slowly rolling up his sleeves. One hand clenched **a** thick willow rod.

"Open the closet, Emma," Semitt said, turning to his wife. "We'll stick her in there when we're through with her."

Mrs. Semitt turned toward a door in the wall, and while the attention of the evil pair was momentarily diverted Nancy reached through the opening and tapped on the desk.

"Sadie!" she whispered.

At the ghost-like voice coming out of thin air Sadie's over-wrought nerves snapped. She screamed and toppled to the floor.

Semitt wheeled and saw the fluttering cloth at the window. With a snarl he rushed forward, his hands thrust out to topple over the ladder on which Nancy swayed.

CHAPTER XXV

THE LAST CLUES

"I'LL agree to call off the suit, if we can come to some agreement," Peter Boonton said to Mr. Drew. "Under the terms of Asa's will, how much does each of our shares amount to?"

"It is hard to say, because the suit has held up the sale of the estate," Mr. Drew replied. "I guess that it will total about two hundred thousand dollars. That will put the individual shares of yourself, your nieces and the others at about thirty-two hundred dollars each."

"What do you say, Jacob?" Peter asked his cousin. "Shall we call quits? That isn't a sum to be sneezed at."

"Come to my office tomorrow and talk it over," Mr. Drew said. "I think the main business now is to find Sadie. Where is Nancy?"

At that moment a muffled scream reached the ears of the four men.

"What was that? It came from the house," Carson Drew exclaimed. "Quick, men! Inside!"

"But how shall we get in?" Jacob cried. "It's all locked!"

"Smash a window," Mr. Drew shouted, as another scream, this one louder and clearer, split the air.

The four men rushed to the front of the mansion and up onto the porch. Mr. Drew snatched up an old folding chair and smashed in one of the window panes. He leaped through the opening, and the others crowded in after the lawyer.

"Upstairs!" Mr. Drew commanded, rushing through the inky darkness toward the hall. Guided only by his memory of the interior and his sense of touch he took the steps two at a time. The other men were not far behind.

Up to the second floor, then up to the Tower Room. Mr. Drew hurled himself forward against the door of Asa's old room, beneath which light gleamed, and the door, unlocked, crashed open.

The four men were confronted by an amazing and uncanny tableau. Nancy Drew's head and shoulders were framed in the window as if she were standing on air. Frank Semitt's arms were thrust through the opening, in the act of pushing Nancy backward into nothingness, and the girl's hands were clutching the evil man's wrists to prevent her from falling.

Clasping her arms around Semitt's waist, and straining to pull him away from Nancy, Sadie Wipple was trying vainly with her puny strength to save her chum and benefactress.

And there, just in the act of bringing down a heavy rod across Sadie's shoulders, stood Emma Semitt!

"Stop!" thundered Mr. Drew, leaping forward. With one sweep of his arm he sent Mrs. Semitt reeling aside. The next instant his hands were gripping Semitt's throat. Mr. Hill quickly reached out to support Nancy, but not a moment too soon, for the crazy old ladder on which she was balanced crashed to the ground below.

Jacob Sidney helped draw Nancy through the window to security, while Peter Boonton guarded the door toward which Emma Semitt had dashed in a hopeless attempt to save herself, regardless of what might befall her husband.

"Let me go!" choked Semitt.

Mr. Drew released the craven inn-keeper, who staggered into a corner, clutching at his throat.

"Are you all right, Nancy?" Mr. Drew asked, turning to his daughter.

"Yes indeed," Nancy answered. "You came just in the nick of time, however. And now let's call the police. I think Semitt and his wife will have plenty to answer for."

"Oh, Nancy, I almost caused you to be hurt," Sadie cried. "It was my scream that revealed you to these people."

"It was what warned us," Mr. Drew said.

"Mr. Boonton, will you take a candle and find the telephone, please? Call the state police headquarters and ask them to send a squad down with the patrol car to take charge of two prisoners."

As Peter hurried off on his errand Nancy turned to Semitt.

"Where is the watchman?" she demanded.

"See if you can find out," was the snarled reply.

"I can answer that," Sadie spoke up. "He forced me to ask the watchman to let us enter again, and the man recognized me, of course. Semitt stayed in the background so the guard would not recognize him, I guess. When the man turned to unlock the door Semitt hit him over the head with something heavy, and tied his arms and legs and then gagged him. He is now in the big clothes closet under the stairs."

"I'll get him out," Jacob Sidney volunteered eagerly, while Semitt darted a hateful look at his late associate in an attempt to break the will.

The guard, shamefaced at having been trapped for a second time, eagerly took charge of the two prisoners, and if Frank Semitt had been left to his mercies he would not have escaped with a whole skin.

"While we are waiting for the police to arrive," Mr. Drew said, sinking into a chair, "let us get to the bottom of this confused state of affairs.''

"First of all, I want to know how Nancy guessed the Semitts would be here,'' Mr. Hill cried. "Did you have some sort of tip they would come back, Nancy?''

''No, I had a hunch that whatever Semitt was after was in the house,'' Nancy said. "And it also seemed to me that Semitt would figure that the old mansion where he had trapped Sadie and me would be the last place anyone would look for him.''

"That is marvelous reasoning,'' Mr. Hill declared. "It certainly was the right solution, but I should never have thought of it.''

"Oh, yes, I am sure you would have,'' Nancy protested.

"I have never had such an exciting time before in my life,'' Mr. Hill said. "Oh, and that reminds me! I received a telegram from New Fernwild—a long one. It is in my office.''

"What did it say?'' Nancy cried eagerly.

"Your other remarkable hunch was well confirmed,'' Mr. Hill said. "Asa Sidney contributed heavily to the orphanage after the second year that little Sadie was sheltered there, and when she was taken by the Semitts Asa Sidney not only pledged himself as reference for them but caused a beautiful playground and swimming pool to be built, to be called the Boonton Memorial Playground!''

"What's all this?" Mr. Drew demanded, sitting bolt upright. "How did you happen to get this information?"

"Just by following Nancy's suggestions," Mr. Hill replied. "It proves, does it not, that Mr. Sidney had some sort of personal interest in Miss Wipple long before she ever saw him?"

"What does it mean?" Sadie cried, looking from one to the other. "Who am I?"

"That is something we do not know yet," Mr. Drew answered, smiling at his daughter with open respect and admiration. "However, I have no doubt that we shall soon learn."

"Perhaps sooner than we expect," Nancy cried, rising and approaching the flat-topped desk on which the great twisted candle burned very low.

With remarkable calm she opened the battered old Bible and extracted the letter which she had been on the verge of reading when Semitt's ruse had interrupted her.

"Here is a letter from the orphanage to Mr. Sidney, dated just before Sadie was taken by the Semitts," she said, opening the envelope and unfolding the sheet inside.

Everyone in the room leaned forward tensely, watching Nancy closely as her eyes scanned the letter. Then she read aloud:

"We beg to enclose all the information available about the child, Sadie Wipple. She was brought to this institution by the rector of St. James's Church into which she had wandered, and because she was not able to speak her name understandably we followed the usual procedure of naming her after one of our contributors.

"Of course, a routine search was made for the child's relatives, and we learned that the baby's mother, a widow named Mrs. John Boonton, had been mortally injured in a street accident from which the little girl had escaped unhurt and in the excitement had wandered away. Efforts to find any relatives of the parents were unsuccessful. They were strangers in the neighborhood, and a search of the meagre belongings gave no trace of their kin."

All eyes were now turned on Sadie, whose own eyes were bright with excitement and joy.

"Then my name is really Boonton!" she exclaimed. "I am related to—to Mr. Asa Sidney's wife! How strange! I wonder what my first name really is—I never cared for Sadie."

"Perhaps this will tell," Nancy said, dramatically touching the spring which caused the secret compartment in the top of the desk to fly open. She drew out the sheets of paper, and with them a thick-barreled fountain-pen concealed inside.

"Nancy, how in the world do you learn such tricks?" Mr. Drew exploded.

"Just by snooping around," Nancy smiled. Then suddenly the happy look faded as she scanned the papers.

They were blank!

"That is certainly strange," Mr. Hill said. "Why should Asa have taken such pains to conceal blank papers?"

"Perhaps he was planning to write something which he wished kept secret," Mr. Drew said, "and the end came before he was able to do it."

Nancy made no comment. She was disappointed, but more than that, she was puzzled. The pen was heavy, and evidently it was filled. In her cogitation Nancy absentmindedly pressed the point of the pen onto one of the blank sheets. What she saw caused her to give a little gasp of surprise. Clear water seemed to flow from the point of the writing instrument.

Just at that moment the police van arrived, with siren wailing and search-lights combing the house. Mr. Drew and Mr. Hill descended to meet the troopers and to join in making the formal complaint against the Semitts, who were guarded on the ground floor by the watchman, Peter, and Jacob.

"Why Nancy," Sadie said, turning to her friend. "Aren't you going down also?"

"No, I am not particularly keen on seeing anyone go to prison," Nancy said soberly.

"The Semitts well deserve it, of course, but I can't be of any use downstairs now. Besides, I have something—very interesting—here."

"Oh, why are you burning up the papers?" Sadie cried. "Is there some bad news on them about me you want kept a secret?"

"There is nothing on the papers anyone can see," Nancy replied. "So far, at any rate."

She held the sheets close to the flame of the twisted candle, scanning them intently as she passed the papers over the flame.

Soon steps were heard on the stairs and Mr. Drew, Mr. Hill and the two middle-aged cousins entered the Tower Room together.

"Now we have nothing further to fear from the Semitts, at any rate," Mr. Drew said with a satisfied sigh of relief. "What in the world are you doing, Nancy?"

"Just a moment, now."

Then she turned to the puzzled group with a radiant face.

"The sheets were inscribed in invisible ink," Nancy announced. "The pen found with the papers seemed to be filled with water, and that gave me a clue. Most invisible inks turn dark under heat—and look!"

She held up the sheets of paper which were now revealed to be partially filled with spidery, old-fashioned writing in what seemed to be rust-red ink.

"That is remarkable," everyone cried.

"Not as remarkable as what it reveals," Nancy exclaimed. "Just listen."

It would be useless to copy here the rather lengthy document that Nancy read to the amazed little group in the Tower Room. In brief, it set forth that Asa Sidney was not yet able to summon courage to openly reveal an old secret, but he hoped that some day the manuscript he was writing in invisible ink would be found and deciphered.

"Perhaps when it is all written I shall be brave and forget the curse I brought upon my family and openly tell what I now put down in secret," read one paragraph of the lengthy introduction.

"Sadie Wipple, whom I intend to make my heir, is the only living person in whom the blood of the Sidneys and the Boontons is united," Nancy read.

A gasp went around the room, and everybody leaned intently forward so as not to lose a word of the astounding revelations. Sadie's face was white.

The manuscript went on to say that Mrs. Boonton's brother, Jeremiah, had two sons, Peter and Arthur.

"That's right," the Peter who was present murmured. "Arthur, poor chap, was killed in the Spanish American War."

Arthur left a son, John, who went to New York to study art. There he met and fell in

love with a young art student, Helen Sidney.
Their relatives forbade a marriage.

At this point in the reading, Jacob Sidney
suddenly buried his face in his hands and
sobbed.

"Go on," he urged. "Don't mind me."

The young couple eloped. Cut off from their
family they started to make their own way.
The following year a baby girl was born. John
Boonton had to find any sort of work he could
to earn a living, and while engaged as a sign
painter he was killed when a scaffold broke and
hurled him to the ground.

"The terrible fate that seems to have followed our family since my own carelessness
took the life of my own baby also took the life
of Helen Sidney Boonton. She was killed in
an accident, and the little girl wandered off,
eventually to be discovered by me in an orphanage under a different name," Nancy read.
"That child, Sadie Wipple, is really Sarah
Sidney Boonton. To shield her from the family feud, I have permitted the secret of her
identity to remain unrevealed, and have en-
trusted her upbringing to my good and faithful
servants, Frank and Emma Semitt, who declare to me that she is being reared as their
own daughter. However, some day Sadie must
learn her true identity if fate is willing. If it
is to be so, then this document will be found
and deciphered."

Utter silence fell over the room.   Then Jacob Sidney arose falteringly and walked over to Sadie—Sarah, now.

"Your mother was my daughter," he said. "You are my grandchild, if you will ever recognize me as your grandfather after the mean way in which I have treated you, Sarah. I sent my daughter Helen out of my life, like a stubborn old fool. I never knew what became of her after she left our home."

A few days later Bess and George and Sadie met at the old house, the former Sign of the Twisted Candles, with Nancy. Together they followed the clues Nancy had established, that every twisted candle marked the spot where Asa had concealed something he treasured.

Family records, old letters, patent papers and yellowed clippings by the score were unearthed, besides many a hoard of coins and banknotes.

"We must leave nothing overlooked, because the property will be sold in a few days under the terms of the will," Nancy said.

"I have been thinking up a plan," Sadie said shyly. "I already have far more money than I can ever use. Suppose I buy the property myself? That will make the shares of the other heirs larger, and at the same time the old homestead will be kept in the family."

"Oh, Sadie dear, what a lovely idea!" Nancy

exclaimed enthusiastically. "And at Thanksgiving you and all the Boontons and all the Sidneys can meet in the old home for the first reunion in fifty years!"

"Which would never have been possible except for you, Nancy," Sadie said gravely.

"No, indeed, without Nancy's guidance from the very beginning the families would still be enemies and the Semitts would have the fortune," George said. "Nancy, I'm glad—ever so glad—we are chums again."

"And I am, too," said Bess, and added laughingly, "It will make it easier, too, for us to watch you solve your next mystery, whatever that will be."

And that is something which all of us, who are also Nancy's chums, are wondering about, ourselves.

THE END

This Isn't All!

Look on the following pages and you will find listed a few of the outstanding boys' and girls' books published by Grosset and Dunlap. All are written by well known authors and cover a wide variety of subjects—aviation, stories of sport and adventure, tales of humor and mystery—books for every mood and every taste and every pocketbook.

THE NANCY DREW MYSTERY STORIES
By CAROLYN KEENE

Illustrated. Every Volume Complete in Itself.

Here is a thrilling series of mystery stories for girls. Nancy Drew, ingenious, alert, is the daughter of a famous criminal lawyer and she herself is deeply interested in his mystery cases. Her interest involves her often in some very dangerous and exciting situations.

THE SECRET OF THE OLD CLOCK
Nancy, unaided, seeks to locate a missing will and finds herself in the midst of adventure.

THE HIDDEN STAIRCASE
Myterious happenings in an old stone mansion lead to an investigation by Nancy.

THE BUNGALOW MYSTERY
Nancy has some perilous experiences around a deserted bungalow.

THE MYSTERY AT LILAC INN
Quick thinking and quick action were needed for Nancy to extricate herself from a dangerous situation.

THE SECRET AT SHADOW RANCH
On a vacation in Arizona Nancy uncovers an old mystery and solves it.

THE SECRET OF RED GATE FARM
Nancy exposes the doings of a secret society on an isolated farm.

THE CLUE IN THE DIARY
A fascinating and exciting story of a search for a clue to a surprising mystery.

NANCY'S MYSTERIOUS LETTER
Nancy receives a letter informing her that she is heir to a fortune. This story tells of her search for another Nancy Drew.

GROSSET & DUNLAP, Publishers, NEW YORK

THE JUDY BOLTON MYSTERY STORIES
By MARGARET SUTTON

Here is a new series of mystery stories for girls by an author who knows the kind of stories every girl wants to read—mystery of the "shivery" sort, adventure that makes the nerves tingle, clever "detecting" and a new lovable heroine, Judy Bolton, whom all girls will take to their hearts at once.

THE VANISHING SHADOW

Judy's safety is threatened by a gang of crooks who think she knows too much about their latest "deal." She is constantly pursued by a mysterious shadow which vanishes before she can get a glimpse of its owner.

THE HAUNTED ATTIC

The Boltons move into a large rambling house reputed to be haunted. Even the brave Judy who has looked forward to "spooky" goings on is thoroughly frightened at the strange scrapings and rappings and the eery "crying ghost."

THE INVISIBLE CHIMES

Through an automobile accident a strange girl is taken into the Bolton household—the whole family becomes attached to her and interested in her story. Judy tracks down many clues before she finally uncovers the real identity of "Honey."

GROSSET & DUNLAP, *Publishers,* NEW YORK